D1241229

JUSTICE LEAGUE
TRINITY WAR

GEOFF **JOHNS** RAY **FAWKES**
JEFF **LEMIRE** J.M. **DEMATTEIS** writers

IVAN **REIS** MIKEL **JANIN**
DOUG **MAHNKE** DANIEL **SAMPERE**
RENATO **GUEDES** FERNANDO **BLANCO**
CHRISTIAN **ALAMY** OCLAIR **ALBERT** ZANDER **CANNON**
KEITH **CHAMPAGNE** VICENTE **CIFUENTES** MARC **DEERING**
EBER **FERREIRA** GENE **HA** JIM **LEE** TOM **NGUYEN**
JOE **PRADO** KENNETH **ROCAFORT** WALDEN **WONG**
SCOTT **WILLIAMS** PATRICK **ZIRCHER** artists

BRAD **ANDERSON** **BLOND** JEROMY **COX** GABE **ELTAEB**
NATHAN **EYRING** **HI-FI** ART **LYON** MARCELO **MAIOLO**
PETE **PANTAZIS** ROD **REIS** ALEX **SINCLAIR** colorists

SAL **CIPRIANO** TAYLOR **ESPOSITO** TRAVIS **LANHAM** ROB **LEIGH**
CARLOS M. **MANGUAL** NICK J. **NAPOLITANO** DEZI **SIENTY** letterers

JIM **LEE**, SCOTT **WILLIAMS** AND ALEX **SINCLAIR** collection cover artists

SUPERMAN created by JERRY **SIEGEL** & JOE **SHUSTER**
by special arrangement with the Jerry Siegel family

Cuyahoga Falls
Library
Cuyahoga Falls, Ohio

EDDIE BERGANZA DAN DIDIO WIL MOSS BRIAN CUNNINGHAM Editors – Original Series
HARVEY RICHARDS Associate Editor – Original Series KATE STEWART Assistant Editor – Original Series
PETER HAMBOUSSI Editor ROBBIN BROSTERMAN Design Director – Books ROBBIE BIEDERMAN Publication Design

BOB HARRAS Senior VP – Editor-in-Chief, DC Comics

DIANE NELSON President DAN DIDIO and JIM LEE Co-Publishers
GEOFF JOHNS Chief Creative Officer
JOHN ROOD Executive VP – Sales, Marketing and Business Development
AMY GENKINS Senior VP – Business and Legal Affairs NAIRI GARDINER Senior VP – Finance
JEFF BOISON VP – Publishing Planning MARK CHIARELLO VP – Art Direction and Design
JOHN CUNNINGHAM VP – Marketing TERRI CUNNINGHAM VP – Editorial Administration
ALISON GILL Senior VP – Manufacturing and Operations HANK KANALZ Senior VP – Vertigo and Integrated Publishing
JAY KOGAN VP – Business and Legal Affairs, Publishing JACK MAHAN VP – Business Affairs, Talent
NICK NAPOLITANO VP – Manufacturing Administration SUE POHJA VP – Book Sales
COURTNEY SIMMONS Senior VP – Publicity BOB WAYNE Senior VP – Sales

JUSTICE LEAGUE: TRINITY WAR

Published by DC Comics. Copyright © 2014 DC Comics. All Rights Reserved.

Originally published in single magazine form as JUSTICE LEAGUE 22-23, JUSTICE LEAGUE OF AMERICA 6-7,
JUSTICE LEAGUE DARK 22-23, TRINITY OF SIN: PANDORA 1-3, TRINITY OF SIN: PHANTOM STRANGER 11,
CONSTANTINE 5, NEW 52 FREE COMIC BOOK DAY SPECIAL 2012 © 2012, 2013 DC Comics. All Rights Reserved.
All characters, their distinctive likenesses and related elements featured in this publication are trademarks of DC Comics.
The stories, characters and incidents featured in this publication are entirely fictional.
DC Comics does not read or accept unsolicited ideas, stories or artwork.

DC Comics, 1700 Broadway, New York, NY 10019
A Warner Bros. Entertainment Company.
Printed by RR Donnelley, Salem, VA, USA. 2/7/14. First Printing.

HC ISBN: 978-1-4012-4519-1
SC ISBN: 978-1-4012-4944-1

Library of Congress Cataloging-in-Publication Data

Johns, Geoff, 1973-
Justice League : Trinity War / Geoff Johns, Jeff Lemire.
pages cm.— (The New 52!)
Summary: "The event that the New 52 has been building towards since the beginning! #1 New York Times best-selling writer Geoff Johns (Green
Lantern, Batman: Earth One) brings together almost two years of plot threads here in Justice League: Trinity War. When the three Justice Leagues
go to war with one another, who's side will everyone be on? Allies will be born, friends will become enemies, and the DC Universe will never be the
same! This hardcover graphic novel collects Free Comic Book Day 2012, Trinity of Sin: Pandora #1-3, Trinity of Sin: Phantom Stranger #11, Justice
League #22-23, Justice League Dark #22-23, Justice League of America #6-7, and Constantine #5"— Provided by publisher.
ISBN 978-1-4012-4519-1 (hardback)
1. Graphic novels. I. Lemire, Jeff. II. Title. III. Title: Trinity War.
PN6728.J87J6558 2014
741.5'973—dc23
2013045590

SUSTAINABLE FORESTRY INITIATIVE
Certified Chain of Custody
At Least 20% Certified Forest Content
www.sfiprogram.org
SFI-01042
APPLIES TO TEXT STOCK ONLY

I WILL NOT BEG, WIZARDS. I *DEFY* THE *AUTHORITY* YOU CLAIM!

DO WHAT YOU WISH TO ME!

BUT IF YOU DO NOT *KILL* ME, I WILL RISE TO POWER AGAIN!

AND YOU WILL FEAR MY NAME AS DOES THE WORLD!

YOU WILL *FORGET* YOUR NAME AS WILL EVERYONE.

I.... AM... YNNN!

MMNFNN!

LET GO OF ME! PLEASE!

YOU WILL FOREVER *QUESTION* YOUR IDENTITY AND FOREVER SEARCH FOR ANSWERS YOU WILL NEVER FIND.

AND *YOU*, PANDORA.

HAVE YOU ANY *SPITEFUL WORDS* FOR US BEFORE *SENTENCING?*

BUT IT'S CLOSE.

THE JUSTICE LEAGUE TOOK DOWN PROFESSOR IVO'S MAD ANDROID, ETTA. THEY DID THEIR JOB.

BUT THEY CAUSED MILLIONS OF DOLLARS IN PROPERTY DAMAGE. THE CITY'S GOING TO SUE *SOMEONE.*

WASHINGTON, D.C.

A.R.G.U.S.
A MILITARY AGENCY CREATED TO COMBAT SUPER-HUMAN THREATS AND SUPPORT THE WORLD'S GREATEST SUPER HEROES, SPECIFICALLY THE JUSTICE LEAGUE.

NO UNAUTHOR PERSONN ALLOWE

WE'VE LOST TRACK OF THE SUPER-HUMAN TEENS LOOSE IN ALASKA, WE'RE AMASSING INFORMATION ON TALIA AL GHUL'S RECRUITMENT ACTIVITIES AND YOUR SISTER CALLED. SHE ASKED IF YOU WERE STILL COMING TO DINNER TONIGHT.

"MAYBE."

YOU'VE CANCELED ON THEM EVERY TIME.

I'VE GOT A *DOZEN* RED LEVEL THREATS BREWING RIGHT NOW, ETTA. WE DON'T HELP CONTAIN THESE AND THEY *ALL* BLOW UP. HOW'S "PROBABLY"?

WE'VE CLEARLY HELPED ESTABLISH *ANY* DAMAGE WAS GREEN ARROW'S FAULT. THE LEAGUE DOESN'T *MAKE* MISTAKES.

I KNOW THEY DON'T, BUT--

WHAT *ELSE*, ETTA?

BETTER, I GUESS.

WHAT'S THIS?

IT CAME FOR YOU THIS MORNING. NO RETURN ADDRESS. NO FINGERPRINTS. NO DNA.

IT'S JUST A BOOK.

LIKE I HAVE TIME TO READ A *MENU.*

COLONEL TREVOR!

YOU'RE USING THE EMERGENCY FREQUENCY. WHAT THE HELL IS IT *NOW?*

WE DON'T KNOW HOW IT'S HAPPENED AGAIN, BUT...

PANDORA'S BOX? WE *CANNOT* LET THAT *OUT* OF HERE!

I KNOW YOU WERE ONE OF THE SOLDIERS WHO HELPED RECOVER IT, COLONEL TREVOR. I KNOW MANY OF YOUR FRIENDS DIED TO CRATE IT UP.

BUT I NEED IT. IT MAY BE THE SOURCE OF MY *CURSE*.

BUT IT'S ALSO THE SECRET TO MY *SALVATION*.

DAMMIT! WHERE THE HELL DID SHE GO? I THOUGHT THERE WAS SOME KIND OF *MYSTICAL SPELL* SEALING THIS ROOM UP!

COLONEL TREVOR?

WHAT?!

DR. STONE IS ON THE LINE. THERE'S BEEN A CYBER ATTACK ON THE RED ROOM.

I WANT A *LOCKDOWN* ON THE *OTHER* ROOMS. ESPECIALLY *THE CIRCUS!*

WE NEED DR. MIST. GET BLACK ORCHID IN HERE, ETTA. AND FIND ME JOHN CONSTANTINE.

MAYBE YOU SHOULD CALL THE JUSTICE LEAGUE, COLONEL? THEY CAN HANDLE *ANYTHING*, RIGHT?

THE JUSTICE LEAGUE...

"IT'S JUST A MATTER OF TIME BEFORE THIS *ALL* COMES CRASHING DOWN."

THE BOX.

THIS TIME I KNOW WHAT I'M DEALING WITH.

AND IT MUST BE DEALT WITH.

EVEN IF IT MEANS THE END OF THE JUSTICE LEAGUE.

YOU'RE JUST A MAN.

THE NEAR FUTURE.

I'M NOT *FRAID* OF YOU, BATMAN. I'M THE *GREEN LANTERN.*

BUT YOU'RE *NO* HAL JORDAN.

F55555

ACID? GIVE ME A BREAK.

YOU *LIED* TO US. *ALL* OF YOU DID. THIS *WAR* IS *YOUR* FAULT.

HEY, *NEW GUY.*

GEOFF JOHNS WRITER

JIM LEE PENCILS 12-16 AND COVER

SCOTT WILLIAMS INKS 12-16 AND COVE

ALEX SINCLAIR COLOR 12-16 AND COVE

KENNETH ROCAFORT ART 5-8 GENE HA ART 7-11

SAL CIPRIANO LETTERER

THAT WAS THE DAY I SAW THE GOLDEN LIGHT TWINKLING IN THE BRUSH. PULSATING, AS IF ALIVE.

WHAT--

WHAT *IS* THIS?

ANH!

THE FOREST SPROUTED OVER THEIR GRAVES, AND GREW, AND *CONSUMED* THEM.

AND WHEN THEY WERE *GONE*, I BEGAN TO *WALK*.

THE LEVANT. 7660 B.C.E.

WADI TAHUNA. 7110 B.C.E.

JAMO. 6970 B.C.E.

AND I BEGAN TO *KNOW* THE WORLD GONE CRUEL WITH SIN.

WHERE *WRATH* STOKED THE FRENZIED FIRES OF HATRED AND VENGEANCE, AND CYCLES OF UNENDING WAR WERE FORGED--

WHERE *ENVY* WHISPERED POISON PROMISES INTO THE EARS OF THE WEAK-WILLED, AND PROSPERITY *CURDLED*--

WHERE *GREED* BROKE THE VALUED BONDS OF NEIGHBORS, AND MATERIAL GOODS GREW PRECIOUS WHILE KINDNESS *DWINDLED*--

AND I COULD NOT STAND IDLY BY.

DEFILER! I'LL *KILL* YOU!

HA! DEAR MOTHER, YOU CAN'T LAY HANDS ON ME. DID YOU NOT *KNOW* THAT?

WE *SINS* ARE YOURS, BUT WE ARE NOT *LIKE* YOU. YOU HAVE *NO* POWER. WE CLAIM *ALL* THERE IS.

DESTI. 6212 B.C.E.

THEY CLAIMED ALL THERE WAS.

UNSEEN, UNKNOWN TO ALL BUT ME, THEY MULTIPLIED THEIR INFLUENCE. THEY FED.

I KEPT ALL I COULD FROM THEM.

MEGIDDO. 6020 B.C.E.

STRUGGLING ALL THE WHILE. SICK ALL THE WHILE, TO FEEL THE SPIRITS OF SIN TRAMPLING THE MORTAL WORLD. MY BODY ACHING. MY INSIDES CLENCHED AND TURNING WITH EVERY STEP.

HUSH NOW. YOU, AT LEAST, WILL LIVE.

KNOWING THAT FOR EACH I COULD SAVE, THEY WOULD CONSUME MULTITUDES.

BUT MY VOW WAS A HELPLESS ONE, AND SHE KNEW IT.

HER MOCKING LAUGHTER ECHOED IN MY EARS FOR CENTURIES. EVEN AS I TRIED TO TURN THE TIDES OF HISTORY AGAINST THE SEVEN.

MEMPHIS, 2620 B.C.E.

MY SUCCESSES WERE SMALL AND FEW. TO A WORLD GROWN RAMPANT WITH SIN, I TRIED TO LEND MY COUNSEL.

ALL TOO OFTEN MY PLEAS FELL ON DEAF EARS. BUT I NEVER ABANDONED HOPE.

EUTOBURG, 9 C.E.

IN TIME, I REALIZED I COULD NOT TEACH THE MORTALS TO RESIST THE TEMPTATION.

BUT IF I COULD NOT TEACH...

ANTRIM, 44 C.E.

...PERHAPS I COULD LEARN.

I WALKED THE DEWY FORESTS OF THE DRUIDS, AND THEY TAUGHT ME TO MAKE AN ALLY OF NATURE.

JERUSALEM, 113 C.E.

I KNELT AT THE DUSTY FEET OF WIZARDS, AND THEY SHOWED ME THE BINDING OF SPIRITS.

NEPAL, 280 C.E.

I SUBMITTED TO THE GENTLE WISDOM OF HEALERS, AND THEY GIFTED ME WITH THEIR MAGICKS.

WHILE THE WORLD FELL FURTHER, HELPLESSLY, INEXORABLY, TO CORRUPTION.

MOUNT SONG, 1328 C.E.

TO MASTER MY PAIN AND CHANNEL IT.

HE SMILED AND TOLD ME THAT "NEVER" IS A LONG TIME.

NO WORDS COULD CONQUER THE SINS. NO MAGIC I FOUND COULD SLOW THEM. IT WAS ON THE SACRED PEAK OF SHAOSHI THAT I FIRST SET ABOUT LEARNING TO FIGHT THEM.

OSAKA, 1418 C.E.

TO DEFY THE LIMITS OF THE PHYSICAL WORLD.

NANTES, 1590 C.E.

TO MOVE FASTER THAN THOUGHT. TO VANISH FROM SIGHT.

FLENSBURG, 1705 C.E.

TO STRIKE THROUGH THE VEIL THAT SEPARATES THE LIVING WORLD FROM THE SPIRITS BEYOND.

KRAK

BOOM

"BLACK ADAM WAS A BAD GUY, BILLY."

I STILL HAVE TO DO *SOMETHING* WITH HIS ASHES, FREDDY.

THIS HOUSE HAS TWO BATHROOMS.

WHICH IS ENTIRELY TOO FEW FOR *SIX* KIDS AND *TWO* ADULTS.

THREE ADULTS IF YOU COUNT BILLY, EUGENE.

YOU MEAN SHAZAM!

NOT SO LOUD, DARLA. MR. AND MRS. VASQUEZ ARE HOME.

BLACK ADAM TRIED TO *KILL* US. WHY WOULD YOU DO *ANYTHING* FOR HIM?

BECAUSE HE DIDN'T GO OFF THE *DEEP END* UNTIL MAGIC CAME INTO THE PICTURE.

YOU'RE NOT GOING TO TURN EVIL LIKE *HIM*, ARE YOU?

NO, DARLA. AND HE WASN'T EVIL. HE WAS MISGUIDED.

WHERE ARE YOU TAKING HIM?

I'LL SPREAD HIS ASHES ACROSS THE KAHNDAQ DESERT.

KAHNDAQ?

THAT'S WHERE HE WAS FROM, MARY.

THAT'S HALFWAY ACROSS THE WORLD.

BILLY CAN *FLY* THERE.

IT'S *DANGEROUS.*

MARY'S RIGHT, BILLY. THE GOVERNMENT HAS ISSUED A *STRICT WARNING* AGAINST *ANY* AMERICAN TRAVELING THERE.

SUPERMAN AND *WONDER WOMAN* WENT THERE TO RESCUE THOSE HOSTAGES LAST WEEK.

BUT *WHY* DO THIS, BILLY?

BECAUSE EVEN "BAD GUYS" DESERVE TO BE BURIED.

"SHAZAM!"

WHAT'S GOING TO HAPPEN TO ME?!

THIS ISN'T ABOUT THE POOR GIRL.

THE HERO

THE WARRIOR

IT'S ABOUT THE JUSTICE LEAGUE.

BELLE REVE PRISON.

I CHANGED OUR TICKETS FOR THE LATER SHOW IF YOU'RE STILL UP FOR IT.

I'D LIKE THAT, BUT I DON'T HAVE FAITH DESPERO'S GOING TO STAY HERE FOR LONG, LET ALONE THE NIGHT.

WHEN HAL SHOWS UP ON EARTH AGAIN, WE'LL ASK HIM TO TRANSFER DESPERO TO OA.

BUT HE'LL EVENTUALLY ESCAPE.

THERE'S A REASON I DON'T HAVE A LIST OF VILLAINS AS LONG AS BRUCE'S, BARRY'S OR EVEN YOURS.

WHEN I DEAL WITH THEM, I DEAL WITH THEM.

I TRUST YOU'RE NOT TALKING ABOUT *KILLING* THEM, DIANA.

ONLY IF IT COMES TO THAT.

THERE'S NO DOUBT *INNOCENT PEOPLE* HAVE BEEN PUT ON *DEATH ROW.*

NOT IF YOU HAVE A *LASSO* OF *TRUTH.*

MAYBE WE SHOULD CHANGE THE SUBJECT.

NO.

FWAP

"NOT *HER.*"

SUPERMAN.

PUT TOGETHER TO SPECIFICALLY COUNTER THE JUSTICE LEAGUE IN EVERY WAY...WITHOUT MOST OF THEIR RECRUITS EVEN REALIZING IT.

IF I *JOIN* THE JLA, THEY'LL HELP ME FIND A *CURE* TO THESE POWERS.

BECAUSE THESE ABILITIES HAVE *DONE* SOMETHING TO ME, KIM.

EVERY ROOM I WALK INTO, I TAKE AWAY THE LIGHT. I *SUCK* IT UP LIKE A *BLACK HOLE.*

I *CRAVE* DARKNESS.

AND NOW THEY WANT ME TO USE THIS POWER AGAINST *FIRESTORM.*

BUT HE'S *ACTUALLY* TWO *KIDS.*

AND THE *LAST THING* I WANT TO DO IS HURT *KIDS.*

"YOU SAID YOU COULD *TRUST* DOCTOR LIGHT, AMANDA, BUT HE'S ALREADY TOLD HIS WIFE EVERYTHING."

WHAT DID YOU DO?

THE BOX...

WHAT'S IT DOING TO HIM?

HE SHOULD HAVE BEEN ABLE TO *OVERCOME* THE INFLUENCE. HE'S *SUPERMAN*.

THERE'S NO *EVIL* IN SUPERMAN!

GET THE BOX *AWAY* FROM HIM, PANDORA.

NOW!

CHAK CHAK

HE'S MORE HUMAN THAN I REALIZED.

"WE'RE ALREADY MAKING A CALL."

YES! WE'RE HEADING INTO KAHNDAQ RIGHT NOW, COLONEL TREVOR.

DOCTOR LIGHT.

GET YOUR HELMET STRAPPED ON AND GET TO THE INVISIBLE JET.

"THE JUSTICE LEAGUE IS HEADING INTO KAHNDAQ.

"IT'S THE JLA'S JOB TO GET THEM OUT."

THE JLA ISN'T READY FOR THIS, WALLER.

THIS IS AN OPPORTUNITY WE MIGHT NOT GET AGAIN, STEVE.

THIS IS OUR CHANCE TO GO SHINE A SPOT-LIGHT ON HOW UNCONTROLLABLE THE JUSTICE LEAGUE IS.

THEY WANT US TO FORCE THE JUSTICE LEAGUE TO DO SOMETHING? THIS IS CRAZY, STARGIRL.

I'M SUPPOSED TO TAKE ON THE FLASH?

WHAT CAN I DO AGAINST CYBORG?

YOU GOT AQUAMAN? YOU DON'T, UH, YOU DON'T WANT TO TRADE DO YOU, HAWKMAN?

NO, VIBE. BUT I'LL TAKE YOURS TOO IF YOU DON'T THINK YOU CAN HANDLE IT.

WHATEVER THEY'RE DOING, IF BATMAN'S INVOLVED, WE SHOULD TRUST THEM.

YOUR PERSONAL INVESTMENT IS CLOUD-ING YOUR JUDGMENT, CATWOMAN.

WHY'S IT GETTING DARK IN HERE?

THIS IS WRONG.

THAT'S WHAT WE CAME TO DO WITH SHAZAM, STEVE.

KAHNDAQ THINKS THEY'RE BEING *INVADED*, DIANA. COME WITH US BEFORE THIS ESCALATES.

THOSE SOLDIERS WERE THE ONES THAT JUST STARTED *FIRING*.

THEN *SUPERMAN* HIT ME.

WHAT WAS I *SUPPOSED* TO DO?

TELL DIRECTOR WALLER AND HER GOVERNMENT WATCHDOGS, THE *JUSTICE LEAGUE* HAS THIS UNDER *CONTROL*. TAKE YOUR "TEAM" *BACK* TO D.C.

AND THIS IS *NO* PLACE FOR YOU, CATWOMAN.

IT'S NOT EXACTLY *YOUR* SCENE EITHER, BATMAN. THOUGHT TRUTHFULLY, I'VE ALWAYS THOUGHT YOU COULD USE A LITTLE MORE *SUN*.

WE'VE GOT THE KAHNDAQ AIR FORCE FLYING OVERHEAD. THIS ISN'T A *JOKE*, CATWOMAN.

OF COURSE IT IS, STEVIE. NOW COME ON. DON'T YOU WANT TO MAKE WONDER GIRL AND BATS A LITTLE *JEALOUS*?

FWAP

I SEE YET ANOTHER PLAYER IN THIS GAME.

ANOTHER MYSTERY.

UNKNOWN

GEOFF JOHNS WRITER **IVAN REIS** PENCILLER

JOE PRADO & **OCLAIR ALBERT** INKERS
ROD REIS COLORS • **DC LETTERING** LETTERS
IVAN REIS, JOE PRADO & **ROD REIS** COVER

I know you probably have a lot of questions.

So do I.

MY FELLOW SOCIETY MEMBERS...

...IT'S TIME.

VLINK

For as long as I can recall, a QUESTION pops into my brain.

Each syllable pounds in my mind OVER and OVER until I find the ANSWER.

"Who is the Hub City Slayer?" was the latest one.

I tracked the killer down and broke both his arms. He confessed and turned himself in.

For a brief moment, I had a reprieve from my haunting headaches.

But soon the next question arrives, kicking and screaming inside my head and demanding an answer.

WHO IS THE EVIL BEHIND THE EVIL?

WHO IS THE EVIL BEHIND THE EVIL

I've been told that someday I'll answer enough questions to get the answer to my own: WHO AM I?

What is my true name?

Until that day comes, I am the Question.

I am the man with no face.

KAHNDAQ.

SUPERMAN

WONDER WOMAN

BATMAN

CYBORG

ELEMENT WOMAN

FIRESTORM

THE ATOM

THE FLASH

ZATANNA

AQUAMAN

SHAZAM

It's a terrible thing to be.

TRINITY WAR

GEOFF JOHNS AND JEFF LEMIRE WRITERS · DOUG MAHNKE PENCIL
CHRISTIAN ALAMY, KEITH CHAMPAGNE, DOUG MAHNKE AND TOM NGUYEN INK
GABE ELTAEB & NATHAN EYRING COLORISTS · ROB LEIGH LETTERER · IVAN REIS, JOE PRADO & ROD REIS CO

THE SKIN AND MUSCLE HAVE ALREADY HEALED, HAWKMAN, BUT IT'S TIGHT BECAUSE IT HEALED *WRONG.*

SO OPEN ME BACK UP AND *FIX* IT.

HERE. USE *THIS.*

I KNOW I'M NEW TO THIS AND MAYBE I'M BEING NAÏVE, BUT SERIOUSLY-- THERE'S *NO WAY* SUPERMAN DID THIS ON PURPOSE.

I'M WITH YOU, LANTERN. SOMEONE'S NOT TELLING US SOMETHING. AND I *HATE* THAT.

DON'T TOUCH THE TRIDENT.

HOW ARE YOU FEELING, FLASH?

STILL A LITTLE *WOBBLY* AND A LITTLE *SLOW.* WHATEVER THAT *VIBE* KID DID TO ME REALLY MESSED ME UP.

CAN YOU BELIEVE THE *BALLS* THESE GUYS HAVE? THEY ACTUALLY *CALL* THEMSELVES THE *JUSTICE LEAGUE* OF AMERICA? *WE'RE* THE *JUSTICE LEAGUE.*

WHO GIVES A CRAP? I'M NOT WITH *EITHER* LEAGUE. CAN I JUST *GO* NOW?

I THINK IT'S BETTER IF YOU STAY, SHAZAM.

YOU CAN'T MAKE ME.

ARE YOU OKAY, RHONDA?

I NEED TO COME CLEAN, ELEMENT WOMAN. I WANT TO TALK TO BATMAN.

BATMAN'S *BUSY,* ATOM.

BUT IF YOU WANT TO TALK TO SOMEONE, I'LL MAKE MYSELF AVAILABLE.

FIRESTORM? I'D LIKE TO SPEAK WITH YOU FOR A MOMENT.

Uh...YEAH? WHAT'S UP?

I NEED TO ASK YOU SOMETHING, AND I NEED A TRUTHFUL ANSWER.

SURE.

CAN YOU MAKE KRYPTONITE?

"HAVE YOU FOUND ANYTHING?"

KER-RANG

When faced with a question, Man tends to gravitate towards logic and science. It makes them feel like they are in control of the things they cannot understand.

But, the real question is, where do gods turn when they can't solve a riddle?

--AK!

D-DIANA?! WHAT THE HELL ARE YOU--

QUIET, HEPHAESTUS! I'M ASKING THE QUESTIONS HERE!

THE BOX, PANDORA'S BOX... WHAT IS IT? *WHAT DOES IT DO?!*

H-HAVE I NOT BEEN YOUR ALLY IN THE PAST, WONDER WOMAN...HAVE I NOT HELPED YOU, AND YET YOU STORM IN HERE AND ATTACK ME LIKE THIS?! IN MY WORKSHOP? MY HOME?

I HAVE *NO TIME* FOR PLEASANTRIES, HEPHAESTUS. IN THE PAST WE'VE BEEN ALLIES, BUT RIGHT NOW I NEED ANSWERS.

PANDORA HAS ACTED RECKLESSLY YET AGAIN, AND THAT DAMN BOX YOU FORGED HAS INFECTED SOMEONE I--

--SOMEONE I CARE FOR DEEPLY.

I NEED TO FIND IT.

I NEED TO KNOW HOW IT WORKS.

YOU ARE THE *WEAPONSMITH OF THE OLYMPIANS.* I KNOW YOU *FORGED* THE BOX.

AND NOW I NEED *THE TRUTH.*

COLONEL TREVOR.

GENTLEMEN.

I NEED TO SEE *SUPERMAN.*

OF COURSE, COLONEL. SHOULD WE--

NO. I NEED TO SEE HIM *ALONE.* I'LL BE FINE. JUST WATCH THE DOOR.

YES COLONEL.

BLEEP

HELLO, SUPERMAN.

KRIK-KSHHH

WHAT ARE YOU DOING?!

YOU *SHOULDN'T* DO THAT...IT'S *NOT SAFE.*

OF COURSE IT IS, SUPERMAN. YOU *ARE NOT* A KILLER.

AND I'M *NOT* STEVE TREVOR...

W-WHO'S THERE?

I'M AFRAID I CAN'T TELL YOU THAT, AT LEAST NOT YET, MADAME XANADU.

I'M SORRY WE HAD TO TAKE YOU LIKE WE DID. YOUR ABILITY TO *SEE THE FUTURE* MAY YET PROVE VALUABLE TO ME. BUT IF LEFT UNCONTROLLED IT COULD RUIN ALL OF MY WELL-PLACED PLANS...

PLANS? AND JUST WHAT ARE THESE GRAND PLANS? WORLD DOMINATION? GAINING UNSPEAKABLE POWER?

WHOEVER YOU ARE, I ASSURE YOU, I HAVE HEARD IT ALL BEFORE. I'M *IMMORTAL*. THERE IS NOTHING YOU CAN POSSIBLY DO THAT *GREATER MEN* HAVEN'T ALREADY TRIED AND *FAILED*.

HEH. MAYBE SO, XANADU. BUT IT'S NOT JUST ME, YOU SEE. THERE ARE *SO MANY* PIECES AT PLAY. THINGS BEYOND YOUR WILDEST IMAGINATION.

SO MUCH HAS HAPPENED SINCE WE DESTROYED YOUR PARLOR AND BROUGHT YOU HERE.

EVEN AS WE SPEAK, THE SCALES ARE TIPPING. SOON IT WILL BE TOO LATE TO STOP WHAT'S COMING.

"YOUR HEROES STILL SCRAMBLE TO MAKE SENSE OF THE BOARD...BUT THE GAME IS ALREADY *WON.*"

A.R.G.U.S. HEADQUARTERS
WASHINGTON, D.C.

FWOOSH

THAT'S *NOT* IT.

YEAH... *I KNOW.* I'LL GET IT.

I STILL DON'T THINK WE SHOULD BE DOING THIS, THOUGH.

REALLY? YOU SAW WHAT SUPERMAN DID TO DOCTOR LIGHT. THERE IS NO WAY OF KNOWING WHAT COULD HAPPEN NEXT.

AND THERE IS *NO WAY* IT WAS SUPERMAN'S FAULT. BATMAN AND THE OTHERS ARE GOING TO FIGURE OUT WHAT REALLY HAPPENED. *WE WON'T NEED THIS.*

YOU DON'T KNOW THAT. *KEEP TRYING.*

FWOOSH

I DID IT!

WE DID IT.

YOU'RE SURE, FIRESTORM? YOU'RE *ONE HUNDRED PERCENT* POSITIVE THAT'S *KRYPTONITE?*

I--I THINK SO.

WE'RE SURE.

NOW WHAT, DIRECTOR WALLER?

NOW YOU WAIT. AND GET READY TO DO IT *AGAIN.*

I'M SORRY, BATMAN. THERE'S NO WAY OF TELLING WHETHER OR NOT DOCTOR LIGHT'S POWER ACCIDENTALLY TRIGGERED SUPERMAN'S HEAT VISION. *NOT EVEN* WITH MAGIC.

PERHAPS NOT, ZATANNA, BUT IT'S STILL THE BEST THEORY WE HAVE.

YOU MEAN OTHER THAN WHAT WONDER WOMAN BELIEVES. THAT PANDORA'S BOX HAS SOMEHOW *CORRUPTED* SUPERMAN? POSSESSED HIM?

UH... GUYS?

WHAT DID YOU DO, ZATANNA?

I DIDN'T DO ANYTHING!

DO NOT BE ALARMED...

TRINITY
WAR
HOUSE OF CARDS

JEFF LEMIRE WRITER   MIKEL JANIN ARTIST
JEROMY COX COLORS • CARLOS M. MANGUAL LETTERS
IVAN REIS, JOE PRADO & ROD REIS COVER

AS WE SPEAK, *WONDER WOMAN* IS IN NEW YORK SEEKING THE ASSISTANCE OF THE MYSTICAL ADVENTURERS YOU MAY KNOW AS THE *JUSTICE LEAGUE DARK.*

SHE HOPES TO RECRUIT THEM TO HELP HER LOCATE A WOMAN NAMED *PANDORA.* IF THEY SUCCEED IT WILL BE THE *DEATH OF ALL.*

MY FATHER TRUSTED HIM, BUT...

BUT SHOULD WE?

IT'S NOT A MATTER OF TRUST, BATMAN. WE CAN'T LET DIANA GET ANYWHERE *NEAR* PANDORA'S BOX.

BUT WHAT IF WONDER WOMAN IS RIGHT, TREVOR? WHAT IF THIS BOX CORRUPTED SUPERMAN?

IT'S TOO *DANGEROUS,* J'ONN. I'VE SEEN WHAT THAT BOX CAN DO. MY FIRST-- AND LAST--MISSION WITH TEAM 7 WAS TO RETRIEVE THE BOX. THE TEAM WAS *DECIMATED.*

CYBORG, CALL FLASH. WE'RE GOING AFTER WONDER WOMAN. BUT I NEED YOU HERE IN CASE SUPERMAN'S CONDITION GETS ANY *WORSE.*

AND I'M LEAVING FIRESTORM, ELEMENT WOMAN AND THE ATOM. THEY ARE NOT READY FOR THIS.

GOT IT.

J'ONN! I'M LEAVING YOU AND GREEN ARROW HERE TO HOLD THE FORT.

THE OTHERS ARE WITH ME.

I WILL CONTINUE THE INVESTIGATION HERE, TREVOR.

YOU HAVE NOT ANSWERED *MY QUESTION*, SUPERMAN...DO YOU WANT TO FIND OUT WHO *REALLY* KILLED DOCTOR LIGHT?

I--I DON'T KNOW HOW YOU GOT IN HERE, OR *WHO* YOU ARE, BUT YOU DON'T SEEM TO UNDERSTAND... ...I DID IT. *I KILLED* DOCTOR LIGHT.

NO, YOU DID *NOT*, SUPERMAN. THERE IS SOMETHING ELSE AT WORK HERE. AND I CAN PROVE IT.

BLEEP BEEP BEEP

DON'T! I CAN'T--

CHAK

IT IS DONE. NOW, THE QUESTION IS, WHAT WILL *YOU* DO NEXT?

WHAT'S THIS?

MAYBE AN *ANSWER*...

SUPERMAN, STOP!

CYBORG, YOU *NEED* TO SEE THIS.

THE QUESTION FOUND THIS. **DR. PSYCHO,** A SUPER VILLAIN KNOWN FOR HIS ABILITY TO CONTROL MINDS, WAS IN KAHNDAQ ONLY *A DAY* BEFORE OUR BATTLE...

THIS IS *IMPOSSIBLE.* I SCOURED EVERY DATABASE ON EARTH FOR ANY INFORMATION ABOUT KNOWN SUPER VILLAINS IN THE AREA.

The Kahndaq Times

Kahndaq Businessman Murdered

Supervillain "Dr. Psycho" wanted for murder of prominent middle eastern real estate magnet.

HOW COULD THIS POSSIBLY HAVE SLIPPED BY ME?

PERHAPS WE ARE LUCKY MY METHODS OF RESEARCH ARE A BIT MORE...*ANALOG,* CYBORG.

CYBORG, *STAND AWAY FROM THE PRISONER.*

WALLER! YOU NEED TO *BACK OFF.* I HAVE THIS *UNDER CONTROL!*

UNDER CONTROL?! SUPERMAN JUST *BROKE OUT* OF HIS CELL.

THE HOUSE OF MYSTERY.

FANCY SEEING YOU HERE, ZEE. I SEE YOU'VE MADE SOME NEW FRIENDS.

DRESSED FOR THE PART TOO, EH, LOVE? AND HERE I WAS HOPING YOU'D COME BACK TO REJOIN *OUR TEAM.*

STEVE, BATMAN, THIS IS RIDICULOUS! YOU TRIED TO DO THINGS YOUR WAY AND IT'S GONE NOWHERE. *SUPERMAN IS DYING.* WE NEED TO FIND PANDORA AND FIGURE OUT WHAT THAT BOX *REALLY IS!*

THAT BOX HAS NOTHING TO DO WITH WHAT'S HAPPENING TO SUPERMAN!

ENOUGH!

DIANA?!

AT LEAST I CAN *TRUST* THE JUSTICE LEAGUE, JOHN. THEY DON'T JUST *PRETEND* TO BE HEROES TO ADVANCE THEIR OWN AGENDA.

OUCH.

YOU SAY THE BOX IS NOT TO BLAME FOR SUPERMAN'S CONDITION? THEN TELL ME, *WHAT IS?*

I-- I DO NOT KNOW.

LISTEN! ALL OF YOU...BATMAN WOULD RATHER TRUST *THIS MAN* WHO CLAIMS TO KNOW EVERYTHING, BUT TELLS YOU *NOTHING.*

WELL, I'M DONE DEBATING. I'M GOING AFTER PANDORA.

SO... WHO'S WITH ME?

SUPERMAN...

I'M--I'M FINE. I'M IN CONTROL.

I'M SORRY, DIRECTOR WALLER, BUT I *AM* GETTING OUT OF HERE. I'M GOING AFTER DR. PSYCHO.

EVERYTHING THAT'S HAPPENED... *WHATEVER'S* HAPPENING TO ME NOW... I *WILL* STOP IT.

SHRACK

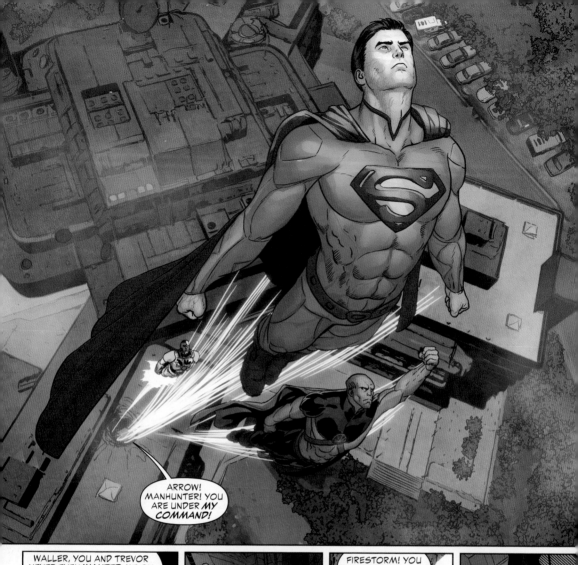

ARROW! MANHUNTER! YOU ARE UNDER *MY* COMMAND!

WALLER, YOU AND TREVOR NEVER EVEN *WANTED* ME ON YOUR DAMNED TEAM. YOU SHUT ME OUT TIME AND TIME AGAIN, AND NOW YOU WANT MY *LOYALTY?*

WELL, I'M SORRY, AMANDA.

ATOM...ARE WE GOING TO GET IN TROUBLE FOR THIS?

ELEMENT WOMAN, I THINK EVERYBODY IS ALREADY IN A WHOLE LOT OF TROUBLE.

FIRESTORM! YOU ARE THE LAST LINE OF DEFENSE. CAN I TRUST YOU?

I--

FIRESTORM!

AH, THERE, WHEN I TOUCHED YOU, YOU SAW SOMETHING, DIDN'T YOU? YOU SAW THE PIECES. YOU SAW THE GAME...

"...YOU SEE, EVEN AS WE SPEAK ALL OF THOSE PLANS ARE BEARING FRUIT. MY PAWNS ARE MOVING UP THE BOARD..."

"THE KNIGHTS ARE MOVING INTO POSITION..."

WE NEED TO GO AFTER WONDER WOMAN.

NO, WE NEED TO TALK TO HIM AND GET ANSWERS.

TALK TO *WHO?*

DOCTOR LIGHT.

DOCTOR LIGHT'S *DEAD.*

YES. HE *IS.*

THIS FIELD OUTSIDE BELLE REVE IS WHERE SUPERMAN CAME INTO CONTACT WITH THE BOX, ZATANNA.

AND I'VE PICKED UP SOME RESIDUAL ENERGY FROM IT.

IS IT ENOUGH TO TRACK PANDORA DOWN?

"...SCATTERED ACROSS THE LANDS..."

"...LEAVING *THE QUEEN* UNPROTECTED."

HA.

I DON'T KNOW WHO YOU ARE, BUT I DON'T NEED TO *SEE THE FUTURE* TO KNOW THE JUSTICE LEAGUE WILL BEAT YOU.

OH, MY DEAR, XANADU, I'M AFRAID YOU ARE VERY WRONG. YOU SEE, WHILE THEY DON'T KNOW IT YET, I'VE *ALREADY* DESTROYED THEM.

The Joint bar

I *KNEW* TONIGHT WAS GOING TO BE A PAIN IN THE ASS.

LIKE, SOME NIGHTS JUST START OUT WRONG AND GET *WORSE.*

PUT CREAM IN MY COFFEE FIRST THING AND IT CAME OUT OF THE CARTON IN *LUMPS.* I SHOULDA GONE RIGHT BACK TO BED.

COME ON, MOPMOP. I CLOSED UP HALF AN HOUR AGO, AND I GOT A REAL UGLY HEADACHE BREWIN' UP. TIME TO GO HOME.

CAN SLEEP HERE. PAPA MIDNITE'S GANG SLEEP WHERE THEY WANT!

NO, NO YOU DON'T. I WORK HARD TO KEEP THIS PLACE RUNNING.

THIS IS *MY* BAR, YOU UNDERSTAND? NOT YOURS, NOT PAPA'S, NOT ANYBODY ELSE'S.

OI, LLOYD. LOCK IT UP.

GONNA NEED THE PLACE FOR A BIT.

EMPLOYERS ONLY

SO THERE I WAS, GOING ABOUT MY BUSINESS, GETTING READY TO STRIKE A BLOW AT THE CULT OF THE COLD FLAME, WHEN I GET THE **CALL.** TROUBLE WITH THE COSTUMES. OF COURSE I'M NOT PREPARED IN THE SLIGHTEST.

NOW I HAVE TO *IMPROVISE.*

ALL RIGHT, CONSTANTINE. YOU SAID YOU HAD SOMETHING I'D WANT TO SEE. SOMETHING TO DO WITH MY REAL *FAMILY.*

SO WHAT IS IT?

THE COSTUMES ARE LOSING IT. SUPERMAN'S ONLY GONE AND KILLED SOMEONE, AND NOW EVERYONE'S FALLING ABOUT LIKE BRIDESMAIDS AT A SHOWER GONE *SOUR*.

I'M GETTING TO IT, MATE.

THIS IS A *DELICATE* TIME, YEAH? AND YOU'RE A VERY IMPORTANT POWER. I'M GOING TO NEED TO KNOW THAT I CAN *TRUST* YOU, BATSON.

IF I'M RIGHT ABOUT HOW THIS IS ALL GOING TO GO, I NEED TO TAKE *BILLY BATSON* HERE OFF THE BOARD RIGHT *QUICK*. IT'S NOT GOING TO LOOK GOOD, BUT YOU KNOW WHAT THEY SAY. BETTER TO BEG *FORGIVENESS* THAN ASK *PERMISSION*.

WHAT'S *THAT* SUPPOSED TO MEAN?

HOW MUCH DO YOU KNOW ABOUT THE POWER YOU WIELD?

MORE THAN *YOU* DO.

I ASK BECAUSE IT'S *MYSTICAL* IN NATURE, AND THE SHAZAM SPELL MAY BE CAUSING *SERIOUS* PROBLEMS.

YOU'LL WANT TO SHUT IT DOWN FOR A MOMENT. TAKE OFF YOUR MAGIC NECK-LACE OR HOWEVER THIS WORKS. I KNOW YOU HAVE ANOTHER *FORM*.

YEAH, RIGHT. WHAT DOES THIS HAVE TO DO WITH MY FAMILY?

WHY SHOULD I TRUST *YOU*?

I'M THE WORLD'S *EXPERT* ON MAGIC, BOSS. I'M THE ONE WHO KNOWS WHAT'S WHAT. BUT I CAN SEE YOU'RE NO SLOUCH YOURSELF. LET ME PUT IT TO YOU THIS WAY. I SENSED A HUGE MYSTIC BUILD-UP WHEN WE WERE BACK IN THE HOUSE OF MYSTERY-- SOME KIND OF *WEAPON* SPELL.

MAYBE A TRAP YOUR FRIEND *BLACK ADAM* SET UP.

IT'S HOMING IN ON YOU RIGHT NOW. I THINK I BOUGHT US ABOUT TWO MINUTES, COMING HERE. YOU KEEP THE POWER RUNNING, AND IT'LL *FIND* YOU, AND POSSIBLY *KILL* YOU. YOU SWITCH YOUR POWER *OFF*, AND IT'LL HAVE NO WAY TO LOCATE YOU. THEN WE NEUTRALIZE IT, SET YOU BACK ON YOUR WAY--

--THEN I TELL THE *JUSTICE LEAGUE* HOW YOU *SELFLESSLY* DREW IT AWAY FROM THEM AND HOW THEY *OWE* YOU A HELL OF A DEBT.

SOMETIMES TRUSTING A *FRIEND* CAN MEAN AN ALL-AROUND WIN, YEAH? ESPECIALLY CONSIDERING THE *ALTERNATIVE*.

UH-OH.

JOHN? WHY DOES HE SOUND LIKE YOU NOW?

IT'S JUST A TRICK. GRAB HIM BEFORE HE GOES ANYWHERE, YEAH?

THIS IS STRICTLY TEMPORARY.

THE BOY AND I ARE SWAPPING *VOICES* FOR A BIT. I SOUND LIKE *SQUEAKY* HERE, HE GETS TO TRY ON ME CHARMING *BARITONE*.

OH, AND I GET TO HOLD ON TO HIS SPECIAL *WORD*.

CHAK

YOU SON OF A--

DC COMICS PRESENTS
CONSTANTINE IN
Stealing Thunder
A
TRINITY WAR
Interlude

RAY FAWKES Writer
RENATO GUEDES Artist
MARCELO MAIOLO Colorist
TAYLOR ESPOSITO Letterer
EDDY BARROWS, EBER FERREIRA
& BRAD ANDERSON Cover

THE POWER... IS AGONY.

SHHZZZTTT

WON'T...BE ABLE TO CONTAIN IT... FOR LONG...

BAM

CRASH
RRAAA

DON'T TOUCH, KID. I DON'T WANT TO HAVE TO HIT YOU. JUST TAKE COVER.

UH, OI!

OI, UGLY! YOU'RE AFTER ME, AREN'T YOU? ...UH, MATEY?

QUITE A TRICK, EH, YA STUPID WANKER? I BLOODY SWITCHED BODIES WITH THE BOY, DIDN'T I?

UH, BOLLOCKS ON YOU! UMM...

THUU ENGLISSHHMANN

BLAM

UUUAAUUU

JOHN--

DON'T *TOUCH* IT, KID. YOU'LL THINK YOU'RE DOING THE RIGHT THING, BUT YOU'LL ONLY *LIGHT* THE *FUSE*.

THIS COMING FROM THE GUY WHO *KIDNAPS* ME, *LIES* TO ME, AND *STEALS* MY POWER.

HOW DO I KNOW YOU'RE NOT TELLING ME THE *OPPOSITE* OF WHAT I SHOULD DO?

I WOULDN'T-- *NNH*--

I WOULDN'T HAVE DONE ANY OF THAT IF I KNEW I COULD *TRUST* YOU. THE POWER YOU HAVE IS *TOO BIG* FOR MAYBES, KID.

RIGHT.

YOU'RE A REAL *JERK*, CONSTANTINE. I HOPE I *NEVER* SEE YOU AGAIN.

>COUGH<

"...AND I'VE OTHER AGENTS WHO NEED TENDING."

TERREBONNE PARISH, LOUISIANA. BELLE REVE PENITENTIARY.

WHAT A WAY TO START THE WEEKEND. WHAT'S THE STORY?

WE'VE GOT ONE *JUSTICE LEAGUE* MEMBER DEAD, AND IT LOOKS LIKE SUPERMAN KILLED HIM, RIGHT? I HAVE A FEELING YOUR WEEKEND BARBECUE PLANS OR WHATEVER HAVE BEEN *DEPRIORITIZED.*

WE'VE GOT SECURITY FOOTAGE OF SUPERMAN AND WONDER WOMAN MEETING UP WITH TH UNIDENTIFIED WOMAN RIGH *HERE* YESTERDAY, AND WE'R READING RESIDUE OF A FRANKLY LUDICROUS ENERGY DISCHARGE AT THIS SPOT.

SENSORS SPINNING ON THEIR DIALS AND BREAKING LIKE SOMETHING OUT OF A SLAPSTICK CARTOON.

SHE'S *NOT* UNIDENTIFIED.

EXCUSE ME?

THIS SAME WOMAN RECENTLY BROKE INTO A SECURE A.R.G.U.S. FACILITY KNOWN AS THE *BLACK ROOM* AND STOLE AN ARTIFACT FROM US. HER CODENAME IS *PANDORA.*

WELL, HOORAY FOR INTERDEPARTMENTAL *COMMUNICATION.* BECAUSE S.H.A.D.E.* HAS BEEN TRYING TO IDENTIFY AND *CLASSIFY* HER HERE.

OKAY, SO YOUR JOB IS DONE. I'M TELLING YOU SHE'S A METAHUMAN THREAT SO SHE'S NOT YOUR PROBLEM.

SPECIAL AGENT *KINCAID,* I'M SPECIAL AGENT *PAUL CHANG,* A.R.G.U.S.* INTELLIGENCE. THIS ONE'S MY JURISDICTION.

HOLD ON. WE HAD ONE OF OUR PSYCHICS HERE AT THE SCENE--HE WENT INTO *CONVULSIONS* THE MOMENT HE STEPPED OUT OF THE CAR.

SAID SOMETHING ABOUT "TEN THOUSAND YEARS OF UNDYING PAIN" BEFORE HE SLIPPED INTO A *COMA.* THE SUSPECT MIGHT BE *PARAHUMAN.*

WOW, A PSYCHIC WITH A *VAGUE* PROCLAMATION AND NO FOLLOW-UP.

I'M *SHOCKED.*

VERY FUNNY. I'LL SAY THIS: I GET THE IMPRESSION JURISDICTION ISN'T QUITE SO CLEAR HERE...

*SUPER-HUMAN ADVANCED DEFENSE EXECUTIVE

*ADVANCED RESEARCH GROUP UNITING SUPER-HUMANS

CHANG, P.
CLEARANCE 3-ULTRA

CRASSSHH

UUGGODD MY EYEEEE...

SIGNALMAN TO COMMAND: WE'RE ENGAGING THE TARGET. GIGANTA IS *DOWN!* I'M SENDING WHATEVER DATA I CAN GATHER ON PANDORA.

I'M READING A COMPOUND FRACTURE ON ONE FEMUR THERE--IT'S ALREADY KNITTING ITSELF BACK TOGETHER.

SKULL FRACTURE TOO, AND A COUPLE OF *VERTEBRAE.* DIDN'T SLOW HER DOWN A BIT, SO WE'RE LOOKING AT PARAHUMAN ENDURANCE AND MOBILITY.

NEUROSCAN SHOWS THAT SHE'S IN *ALL KINDS* OF PAIN, BUT SHE'S JUST-- GOD, SHE'S JUST CARRYING IT.

VAPOR ANALYSIS OF THE *SMOKE* SEEMS TO INDICATE THAT SHE'S NOT *BREATHING.*

SOME KIND OF MYSTIC ENERGY SIGNATURE ON HER WEAPONS, BUT ONLY WHEN SHE'S *HOLDING* THEM.

EXPLOSIVE IN THE HILT ON THE BLADES, AND INDICATION THAT SHE DOESN'T NEED TO ACTUALLY *SEE* TO HIT HER TARGET.

SAVAGE IS MOVING IN TO ENGAGE.

RRRAH!

UNGH!

HEH. YOU THINK YOU CAN STOP ME? YOU KNOW I'M NOT LIKE ANYONE ELSE. *NOTHING* CAN STOP ME.

REALLY?

BLAMM

YOU... YOU... YOU *KILLED* HIM.

HE WOULDN'T STOP. HE WOULDN'T *LISTEN*.

AND THIS IS USEFUL TO ME *HOW?*

I'M SORRY, SIR, BUT I DON'T SEE HOW--

BUT I--

BUT--

--SIGH-- OKAY, AS OF NOW, THIS IS AN *INTERDEPARTMENTAL* OPERATION. LOOKS LIKE WE'RE WORKING TOGETHER ON THIS.

OH GOODY.

YEAH, WE'RE GOING TO HAVE *SO* MUCH FUN. JUST BE GLAD THEY'RE NOT BRINGING THE D.E.O. IN ON THIS TOO.

I'VE GOT ORDERS FOR TOTAL DISCLOSURE. CANCEL *YOUR* BARBECUE PLANS OR WHATEVER, AGENT KINCAID--YOU'VE GOT A LOT OF READING TO DO.

THERE ARE FILES ON PANDORA THAT MAKE THE PHONE BOOK LOOK SKINNY. SIGHTINGS THAT DATE BACK TO *THE CRUSADES.*

NO KIDDING? WHAT'S A *PHONE BOOK?*

LOOK, IF THIS IS ALL REALLY HER, SHE'S JUST *OLD.* S.H.A.D.E. IS EQUIPPED TO HANDLE THE UNDEAD. IT TAKES THE RIGHT TOOLS, THAT'S ALL.

SO BOIL IT DOWN FOR ME, AGENT CHANG--IS SHE A *GHOST?* A *VAMPIRE?*

SHE MAY OR MAY NOT BE THE PANDORA OF ANCIENT MYTH. YOU KNOW, THE ONE WHO OPENED THE URN OF THE GODS AND SET LOOSE ALL THE EVILS OF THE WORLD?

UH-*HUH.*

AND SHE M OR MAY NOT *SANTA CLAUS* A MAGIC SO PUPPET.

I'M ASKING YO IF YOU KNC WHAT SHE *IS.*

YOU TELL ME--YOU'RE THE *PARAHUMAN* EXPERT. HERE'S EVERYTHING WE'VE GOT.

YOU SERIOUSLY STILL USE PAPER.

I PREFER IT. AND IT MIGHT BE A GOOD IDEA TO READ *ALL OF IT.* A.R.G.U.S. COULDN'T KEEP HER OUT OF THE MOST SECURE FACILITY IN THE WORLD, AND *MAXIMUM FORCE* FAILED TO BRING HER DOWN ON HER WAY BACK *OUT.*

AND AN EXECUTIVE ORDER JUST CAME IN, STRAIGHT FROM THE *TOP.*

AS OF RIGHT NOW, PANDORA IS PRIORITY TARGET *ONE* FOR BOTH OUR AGENCIES.

ALL AVAILABLE RESOURCES ARE DIVERTED TO THIS MISSION. NO DELAYS, NO EXCUSES. THE TARGET IS TO BE *LIQUIDATED* WITH ABSOLUTE PREJUDICE.

THEY SEEM MORE INTERESTED IN WHAT LIES BELOW, *DEADMAN*--THAN IN US.

TAKE ANOTHER LOOK, *KATANA.*

WE'VE GOT TO *LEAVE.* NOW.

ENTITIES LIKE THIS HAVE BEEN INVADING MY LIFE FOR *YEARS* NOW. THE BEST WAY TO DEAL WITH THEM IS TO *STAY*--

--AND SHOW THEM WHAT THE *LIVING* ARE CAPABLE OF!

THESE AREN'T THE DEAD YOU'RE *ACCUSTOMED* TO, KATANA. GIVEN THE CHANCE, THEY'LL DRINK DEEPLY AT THE *WELL OF OUR SOULS*--

--SUCKING OUT EVERY LAST *DREAM* AND *DESIRE...EVERY THOUGHT* AND *FEELING*--UNTIL WE'RE *HOLLOWED OUT*--

SHRAKK

--AND LEFT *LESS* THAN DEAD.

IF WE *LET* THEM!

NO! DON'T *ENGAGE* THEM!

WHAT? WHY?

THIS IS A *BREAKING AND ENTERING JOB,* KATANA--AND THE *LAST* THING WE WANT TO DO--

--IS DRAW THE *ATTENTION* OF THE LOCAL *AUTHORITIES.*

THE QUICKER WE CAN MOVE *THROUGH* HERE AND ON TO THE *NEXT LEVEL* OF THE AFTERLIFE--

--THE LESS OF A CHANCE THAT WE'LL BE *NOTICED.*

CONSIDERING THIS PLACE IS RUN BY A GUY WHO'S *OMNIPOTENT* AND *OMNIPRESENT*--

--I DON'T REALLY SEE IT *HAPPENING!* THAT *SAID*--

--I'VE GOT AN *IDEA!*

COME ON, YOU HUNGRY BASTARDS--YOU WANNA FEED ON SOMEONE--

--*FEED ON ME!*

BRAND-- *NO!* DIDN'T YOU HEAR WHAT THE STRANGER *SAID?* THEY GET THOSE TENTACLES *INTO* YOU AND--

AND...?

WHAT HAPPENED?

THESE SOULS GAIN STRENGTH... PURPOSE...FROM FEEDING ON THE *LIVING.* FEEDING ON A *GHOST* HAS THE...*OPPOSITE* EFFECT.

WHICH IS WHY I *PUT* THE IDEA IN BRAND'S MIND IN THE *FIRST* PLACE.

GOOD THING IT *WORKED...* OR I'D BE *SERIOUSLY* PISSED.

I ASSUME THEY'LL REVIVE *QUICKLY...?*

CORRECT.

AND A DEEPER *FEAR*.

...I CAN'T BELIEVE *YOU*, OF ALL PEOPLE, ARE *SUGGESTING* THIS.

BUT ISN'T THIS KIND OF THING YOUR *STOCK IN TRADE*?

A FEAR I UNDERSTOOD ALL TOO *WELL*.

THE AFTERLIFE IS FOR THE *DEAD*, BATMAN--NOT THE *LIVING*. AND...AS I'VE *RECENTLY* LEARNED--

--IT'S *BEST* TO LEAVE THE DEAD *ALONE*.

AN *HOUR* AGO--OR PERHAPS IT WAS AN *INSTANT* (IMPOSSIBLE TO TELL WHEN YOU'RE AT THE *CROSSROADS OF TIME AND SPACE*)...

...WE STOOD WITHIN *THE HOUSE OF MYSTERY*...

DOCTOR LIGHT IS DEAD, STRANGER. *KILLED*--OR SO MOST PEOPLE BELIEVE--BY *SUPERMAN*.

THAT SINGLE EVENT TRIGGERED A *CHAIN REACTION* THAT'S RIPPLED ACROSS THE *WORLD*. BROUGHT THREE *JUSTICE LEAGUES* TO *WAR*--AND THEN UNEASY *PEACE*.

...PONDERING THE *IMPOSSIBLE*.

I KNOW THAT SUPERMAN'S NOT RESPONSIBLE--

--AND I'M WILLING TO BET THAT *LIGHT* DOES, TOO.

IF WE CAN *INTERROGATE* HIM...GET SOME EVIDENCE THAT WILL LEAD US TO THE ONES *BEHIND* THIS, THEN--

I'M *SORRY*, BATMAN--BUT THE ANSWER IS *NO*.

DON'T TURN YOUR *BACK* ON ME--

AND DON'T *YOU* MEDDLE IN THINGS THAT ARE BEYOND YOUR *PATHETICALLY LIMITED* COMPREHENSION!

I'M... *SORRY*.

THERE'S *SOMETHING* YOU'RE NOT *TELLING* ME--

THERE WERE *MANY* THINGS I WASN'T TELLING HIM.

HOW I'D JOURNEYED FROM THE BOWELS OF *HELL* TO THE HEIGHTS OF *HEAVEN* IN SEARCH OF MY MURDERED *WIFE* AND *CHILDREN*.

HOW I'D *LOST* THEM...

...AND BEEN WARNED BY THE ANGEL *ZAURIEL* NEVER TO *RETURN* TO THE AFTERLIFE.

"IF YOU SO MUCH AS *ATTEMPT* IT," HE SAID...

..."YOU WILL BE *ERASED* FROM TIME AND HISTORY."

WE *ALL* HAVE OUR SECRETS.

I ASK THAT YOU RESPECT *MINE*.

FAIR ENOUGH. BUT I ASK *YOU* TO THINK ABOUT A MAN WHO *EMBODIES* HOPE.

WHO'S *SACRIFICED* HIMSELF AGAIN AND AGAIN FOR THE *GREATER GOOD*.

YOU SPEAK OF SUPERMAN AS IF HE'S SOME KIND OF... *MESSIAH*.

NO. FOR ALL HIS POWER...HE'S JUST A *MAN*. BUT A *GOOD* MAN--

--WHO NEEDS YOUR *HELP*.

STRANGE AS IT SOUNDS, I COULD FEEL THE HOUSE *COME AWAKE* AROUND US...

...EAGER AND INTERESTED...LIKE A VITAL *LIVING THING*.

WAS IT, I WONDERED, MERELY *REFLECTING* OUR THOUGHTS AND FEELINGS...

TELL ME ABOUT THE *VICTIM*. WHO IS THIS...*DOCTOR LIGHT*?

...OR SUBTLY *INFLUENCING* THEM?

FROM ALL I'VE LEARNED, *HE* WAS A GOOD MAN, *TOO*. PULLED INTO *AMANDA WALLER'S* *J.L.A.* AGAINST HIS WILL--

BUT WHY *THIS* PLACE...?

PERHAPS THESE SOULS THINK THEY DON'T *DESERVE* ANYTHING BETTER. OR PERHAPS *HALLS OF GOLD* AND *HEAVENLY CHOIRS* AREN'T FOR EVERYONE.

HEAVEN IS A *RELATIVE* CONCEPT, AFTER ALL.

EXACTLY.

IN THE END, THIS IS JUST A *TRANSITIONAL REALM.* THE ANGELS WILL EVENTUALLY MOVE ALL OF THESE SPIRITS INTO THE *DEEPER* AFTERWORLDS.

WHAT ABOUT *LIGHT?* IS *HE* HERE?

NO. I'D *KNOW* IT IF HE WAS.

WHICH MEANS WE HAVE TO LOCATE THE *SPECIFIC* HEAVEN--

--THAT HE'S *CREATED* FOR HIMSELF...

WHAT DID YOU SAY, BATMAN?

BATMAN?

GONE. DEADMAN AND KATANA GONE *WITH* HIM. AND IN THAT MOMENT I REALIZED THE TERRIBLE *MISTAKE* I'D MADE.

IN A PLACE WHERE *MIND* CREATES MATTER, WHERE THE INDIVIDUAL *HEART* INSTANTLY MOLDS ITS OWN *PARADISE...*

...I SHOULD [HA]VE FORESEEN [TH]AT *EACH OF THEM...*

...WOULD BE SWEPT OFF INTO A HEAVEN OF THEIR *OWN* MAKING.

MASEO?

SURPRISED TO SEE YOUR *DEAD* HUSBAND, *TATSU?*

EVEN A GHOST WHO ROAMS THE EARTH NEEDS A PLACE TO *REST.* SO, FROM TIME TO TIME, I *RETREAT* TO WHAT YOUR FRIEND CALLED...HEAVEN'S BASEMENT.

I CAN'T SAY I CARE FOR THE *NATIVES...* BUT, FOR THE MOST PART, THEY LEAVE ME *ALONE.*

WHEN I SAW *YOU* THERE AMONG THEM, I TOOK A RISK...*FOLLOWED* YOU--

--KNOWING THAT...*TOGETHER*... OUR LOVE WOULD CREATE A *HAVEN* FOR US TO SHARE.

AND HERE WE *ARE.*

FOR *HOW LONG?*

TIME HAS *NO MEANING* HERE.

BUT--

WHY *QUESTION,* TATSU. WHY *OBJECT?*

YOUR LIFE ON EARTH IS A *LIVING HELL* OF PAIN AND SORROW. ENDLESS VIOLENCE.

PUT IT ALL *ASIDE,* MY LOVE--

--AND EMBRACE *HEAVEN.*

NO. YOU RESIST ME. DOES YOUR GUILT...INHIBIT YOU?

YOU *KNOW.*

OF YOUR... *DALLIANCE* WITH MY BROTHER? THE VERY MAN WHO *MURDERED* ME?

IT'S NOT THAT *SIMPLE.*

BUT IN THIS GARDEN--*IT IS.*

TAKEO IS WORLDS AWAY.

HERE YOU ARE FREE TO *LOVE* ME, TATSU.

I...*DO,* MASEO. I--

BACK, WRAITH!

RUMMMMMM

BACK TO THE *LOWER REGIONS* WHERE YOU *BELONG!*

MASEO!

WHAT HAVE YOU DONE TO MY *HUSBAND?*

WHAT HAVE YOU DONE?!

HOW CAN YOU BE SURE THAT *WAS* YOUR HUSBAND?

I KNOW MASEO BETTER THAN I KNOW *MYSELF!*

PERHAPS IT WAS. OR PERHAPS HE WAS A *PROJECTION* OF YOUR OWN DESIRE.

OR...WORSE...ONE OF THOSE *BASEMENT-DWELLERS...* *MANIPULATING* YOU--IN ORDER TO *FEED* ON YOUR LIFE-FORCE.

IN *ANY CASE--*

--HE WAS A *DISTRACTION* FROM THE MISSION AT HAND.

YOU HAD NO *RIGHT* TO TAKE HIM FROM ME! *YOU HAD NO--*

SHHHKK

--*RIGHT!*

CHOK!

FORGIVE ME.

I'M THE ONE WHO NEEDS FORGIVENESS. I SHOULD HAVE *KNOWN* THIS WOULD HAPPEN.

WHERE ARE THE *OTHERS*?

I'M NOT SURE ABOUT *BRAND*...BUT IT WON'T BE DIFFICULT--

"--TO FIND *BATMAN*."

"...MARLEY WAS DEAD: TO BEGIN WITH. THERE IS NO DOUBT WHATEVER ABOUT THAT. THE REGISTER OF HIS BURIAL WAS SIGNED BY THE CLERGYMAN, THE CLERK, THE UNDERTAKER, AND THE CHIEF MOURNER.

"SCROOGE SIGNED IT: AND SCROOGE'S NAME WAS GOOD UPON 'CHANGE, FOR ANYTHING HE CHOSE TO PUT HIS HAND TO. OLD MARLEY--

"--WAS AS DEAD AS A DOORNAIL.

"MIND! I DON'T MEAN TO SAY THAT I KNOW, OF MY OWN KNOWLEDGE, WHAT THERE IS PARTICULARLY DEAD ABOUT A DOORNAIL. I MIGHT HAVE BEEN INCLINED, MYSELF, TO REGARD A COFFIN-NAIL AS THE DEADEST PIECE OF IRONMONGERY IN THE TRADE.

"BUT THE WISDOM OF OUR ANCESTORS IS IN THE SIMILE; AND MY UNHALLOWED HANDS SHALL NOT DISTURB IT, OR THE COUNTRY'S DONE FOR. YOU WILL THEREFORE PERMIT ME TO REPEAT, EMPHATICALLY, THAT MARLEY WAS AS DEAD AS A DOORNAIL."

IT'S GETTING LATE, *THOMAS*. I THINK WE SHOULD GET *BRUCE* TO BED.

BUT HE JUST *STARTED* THE STORY!

YES. FOR THE *SECOND* TIME.

PLEASE, MOTHER...?

÷SIGH÷ *FIVE* MORE MINUTES--

"SCROOGE KNEW HE WAS DEAD? OF COURSE HE DID. HOW COULD IT BE OTHERWISE? SCROOGE AND HE WERE PARTNERS FOR I DON'T KNOW HOW MANY YEARS..."

WHERE *ARE* WE?

A PLACE THAT *NEVER WAS.* A *CHRISTMAS* THAT NEVER HAPPENED.

THAT LITTLE BOY ONCE SPENT THIS HOLIDAY *GRIEF-STRICKEN* AND *ALONE.* BUT HERE HE CAN *REWRITE HISTORY.* HERE--

"--CHRISTMAS CAN LAST *FOREVER.*"

"SCROOGE WAS HIS SOLE EXECUTOR, HIS SOLE ADMINISTRATOR, HIS SOLE ASSIGN, HIS SOLE RESIDUARY LEGATEE--

"--HIS SOLE FRIEND AND SOLE MOURNER."

ARE YOU SAYING THAT THE BOY ON THE *COUCH*--

--IS *BATMAN?*

IS IT SURPRISING THAT A MAN WHO LIVES WITH DARKNESS AND BRUTALITY *DAY AFTER DAY*--

--WOULD SEEK REFUGE...FIND *HEAVEN*--

--IN A BOY'S LOST *DREAMS?*

NOT SURPRISING AT *ALL.*

AND MAYBE *ONE* DAY...WHEN I'M GIVEN THE CHANCE TO *REST*...I'LL COME *BACK* HERE.

BATMAN? THEN THAT'S *NOT...?*

HE'S A *PART* OF ME, KATANA--*THEY'RE* A PART OF ME--THAT I WANTED TO GLIMPSE...FOR JUST A *MOMENT.*

"AND EVEN SCROOGE WAS NOT SO DREADFULLY CUT UP BY THE SAD EVENT, BUT THAT HE WAS AN EXCELLENT MAN OF BUSINESS ON THE VERY DAY OF THE FUNERAL--

"--AND SOLEMNIZED IT WITH AN UNDOUBTED BARGAIN."

BUT THAT MOMENT HAS *PASSED.*

MY *APOLOGIES,* KATANA-- BUT, IN ORDER TO PROTECT BATMAN'S IDENTITY, I MUST...*DIM* THE MEMORY OF THIS ENCOUNTER.

WHAT ENCOUNTER?

HAVE YOU LOCATED *DOCTOR LIGHT?*

NOT *YET,* BUT--

BUT *I* HAVE!

BRAND?

WHILE *YOU* WERE ALL PLAYING "BUILD-A-HEAVEN," *I* WAS OUT SCOURING *EVERY CORNER* OF THIS PLACE.

BUT HOW WERE YOU ABLE TO *RESIST* THE PULL OF--

EASY. I DID SOME PRETTY ROTTEN THINGS WHEN I WAS ALIVE--AND THE *POWERS-THAT-BE* GAVE ME A *SECOND CHANCE.*

THAT CHANCE IS BACK IN THE LAND OF THE *LIVING*-- NOT *HERE.*

--LOST IT...? WHERE... WHERE *ARE* WE?

PRETTY *SPECTACULAR*--

GUESS YOU COULD SAY I'M MORE INTERESTED IN *AVOIDING HELL* THAN *GAINING HEAVEN.*

WHAT ABOUT *YOU,* STRANGER?

I FOUND MY PARADISE ON *EARTH,* DEADMAN. FOUND IT, LIVED IT, AND--

--ISN'T IT...?

THERE IS A *TRANQUILITY* HERE...AN ABSOLUTE *SERENITY*...THAT I HAVE NEVER *FELT* BEFORE.

MAKES A STRANGE KIND OF *SENSE* THAT A MAN WITH THE POWER TO *BEND LIGHT* AND *MANIPULATE ENERGY*--

--WOULD CREATE A *PERSONAL UNIVERSE COMPOSED* OF LIGHT.

IF HE DID...HE DID IT *UNCONSCIOUSLY.*

LOOK AT HIM-- HE'S NOT *AWAKE.* NOT *AWARE.*

--WHERE HIS CONSCIOUSNESS CAN TRANSITION *GENTLY* BETWEEN THE WORLDS--AND *MAKE PEACE* WITH WHAT'S HAPPENED.

GONNA MAKE HIM KINDA HARD TO *INTERROGATE.*

WE KNOW WHAT WILL HAPPEN IF WE *DON'T!* WHILE LIGHT FLOATS ALONG IN HIS *PERSONAL HEAVEN*--

--*MY FRIEND* IS BURNING IN AN *UNDESERVED HELL!*

WHY *NOT?*

THINK ABOUT IT. THE MAN WAS *MURDERED*--SUDDENLY AND UNEXPECTEDLY. TORN FROM HIS LIFE WITHOUT *WARNING.*

THIS PLACE...IS A KIND OF *WOMB*--

THEN WE WAKE HIM UP.

WE DON'T KNOW WHAT COULD HAPPEN IF WE TEAR HIM *OUT* OF THERE.

WE CAME HERE TO HELP *SUPERMAN*--

NO! *NO!* OH, *GOD*--IT HURTS!

IT HURTS!!!

NO ONE WILL HURT YOU *ANY MORE*, ARTHUR. I PROMISE.

I *PROMISE.*

I'M-- I'M *DEAD.*

YES. BUT DEAD OR *NOT*--WE NEED YOUR *HELP.*

WHAT DO YOU *REMEMBER,* ARTHUR... ABOUT WHEN YOU *DIED?*

WE *KNOW* SUPERMAN WASN'T *RESPONSIBLE*... SO WHO *WAS?* IF YOU HAVE *ANY* IDEA...ANY *CLUE*--

HOW...HOW *COULD* I? IT ALL HAPPENED SO *FAST.* SUDDENLY... I WAS *BURNING...* AND THEN--

YOU MUST REMEMBER *SOMETHING!*

I...I WISH I *DID,* BUT--

DON'T LIE TO ME, LIGHT! *DON'T--*

BATMAN... HE DOESN'T *KNOW.*

THEN I'VE *FAILED* SUPERMAN. AND ALL THIS--

--WAS FOR *NOTHING.*

NO. THERE'S *STILL* A WAY.

IF WE TAKE LIGHT *BACK* WITH US...RETURN HIM TO *LIFE--*

--THEN THERE *NEVER WAS* A MURDER. SUPERMAN... IS *FREE.*

AND *YOU,* ARTHUR--

--YOU'LL HAVE YOUR *FAMILY* BACK.

NOTHING--IN LIFE OR DEATH--IS MORE IMPORTANT THAN *THAT.*

IS...IS IT *POSSIBLE?*

NO--

--BUT WE'LL DO IT *ANYWAY.*

BRING THE DEAD-- *BACK TO LIFE?*

THAT'S *INSANE.*

I *LIKE* IT.

STRANGER...IF THIS *DOESN'T WORK...* IF YOU CAN'T GET ME *HOME*--

I CAN. I *WILL.*

I DON'T DOUBT YOUR *INTENTIONS.* BUT INTENTIONS AREN'T ALWAYS *ENOUGH.*

SO *TAKE* THIS... *PLEASE*--

--AND *PROMISE ME* THAT...IF WE *FAIL...* YOU'LL BRING IT TO MY WIFE AND CHILDREN--

--AS A *FINAL GIFT...*

YOU HAVE MY *WORD.*

BUT *LISTEN* TO ME, ARTHUR: WE'RE NOT *GOING* TO FAIL.

LISTEN TO *ME,* STRANGER.

YOU WERE *WARNED,* STRANGER, *NEVER* TO RETURN HERE.

YOU *KNEW* THAT ANOTHER ATTEMPT TO RETRIEVE A SOUL FROM THE AFTERWORLDS WOULD RESULT IN YOUR *EXTINCTION.*

HIS *EXTINCTION...?*

HEY! HEY...WAIT A MINUTE! YOU CAN'T *DO* THAT!

STRANGER-- WHY DIDN'T YOU *TELL* US? WE--

YOU THREE HAVE DONE *ENOUGH* DAMAGE.

BEGONE.

PLEASE-- HE WAS ONLY TRYING TO *HELP.*

YOU CAME HERE TO *REST,* ARTHUR LIGHT. TO *HEAL.* SO LET HEAVEN *NURTURE* YOU--

--AND LET *ME* SEE TO THE PHANTOM STRANGER.

WHY *DIDN'T* YOU TELL THEM? AND WHY DID YOU *DO* IT? RISK ALL *YOU ARE* FOR PEOPLE YOU HARDLY KNEW.

I HAD NO *ANSWER.* IT WAS--AS THE ANGEL SAID--A *FOOLISH* ACT.

BUT, ONCE, TWO THOUSAND YEARS AGO, I *SERVED* A MAN THAT SOME CALLED A FOOL.

I KNEW THE *RISKS*, ZAURIEL. IF THE PRICE I PAY FOR WHAT I DID HERE TODAY IS TO HAVE MY EXISTENCE *ERASED* FROM TIME AND MEMORY-- --THEN *SO BE IT.*

AND I THINK, PERHAPS, THAT HE MIGHT BE *PLEASED...*

...BY WHAT I DID HERE TOD--

A FOOLISH MAN

J.M. DEMATTEIS writer
FERNANDO BLANCO artist
BRAD ANDERSON colorist
TRAVIS LANHAM letterer
GUILLEM MARCH cover

THEY SAY I'M A BAD MAN.

AS IF PEOPLE WERE AS EASILY DEFINED AS NIGHT AND DAY.

CHARGES OF FRAUD AND CONSPIRACY WILL ALSO BE DROPPED, MR. LUTHOR.

WE COULD HAVE YOU OUT OF HERE AS EARLY AS TONIGHT.

I SUPPOSE THAT'S WHAT SIMPLER MINDS NEED TO DO TO CONVINCE THEMSELVES THEY UNDERSTAND HOW THE WORLD WORKS.

MR. LUTHOR?

THEY PUT THINGS IN COLUMNS OF GOOD OR EVIL.

LIKE CHILDREN.

I'VE NEVER LIKED CHILDREN.

MR. LUTHOR, WE'RE TALKING ABOUT FINALLY GETTING YOU OUT OF HERE A FREE MAN.

YOU'LL REGAIN FULL CONTROL OF LEXCORP.

YOU WILL HAVE YOUR LIFE BACK, SIR.

WHAT'S IN THE NEWSPAPER THAT'S MORE IMPORTANT THAN THAT?

DAILY PLANET
SUPERMAN ACCUSED OF MANSLAUGHTER
Newest Member of the JLA Dead

IF EVERYONE SAW THE WORLD THE WAY I DO, THEY'D KNOW WHY I HATE IT SO MUCH.

I HAVE DISSECTED THE MINDS OF *PRIESTS, SOCIAL ACTIVISTS* AND *PHILANTHROPISTS.*

I HAVE SEARCHED FOR YEARS FOR SOMEONE THAT IS FREE OF *SELFISHNESS, HATE* AND *PERVERSION.*

BUT *NO ONE* IS *UNSULLIED.* NO ONE IS WITHOUT *EVIL* THOUGHTS.

P-PLEASE, LET US GO. PLEASE, DON'T KILL US!

I'M NOT GOING TO KILL YOU, MY DEAR.

IT ONLY TAKES THE *SLIGHTEST* TELEPATHIC PUSH FOR MOST PEOPLE.

YOU *UGLY* PEOPLE WHO THINK *UGLY* THOUGHTS.

NOW YOU'LL DO *UGLY* THINGS.

DOCTOR PSYCHO!

NNGG!

KRRNNGG

YOU'RE GOING TO KILL *EACH OTHER.*

AND YOUR THOUGHTS ARE AS CLEAR TO ME AS THEY ARE TO GOD.

IF SUCH A *FAIRY TALE* EXISTED.

NO. THE MARTIAN.

HE'S FOUND ME.

GEOFF JOHNS AND JEFF LEMIRE WRITERS
DOUG MAHNKE PENCILLER
CHRISTIAN ALAMY, KEITH CHAMPAGNE,
MARC DEERING, DOUG MAHNKE & WALDEN WONG INKERS
NATHAN EYRING, PETE PANTAZIS
& GABE ELTAEB COLORISTS · ROB LEIGH LETTERER
DOUG MAHNKE AND ALEX SINCLAIR COVER

C'MON, RING!

DO NOT EMBARRASS ME IN FRONT OF EVERYONE AGAIN.

KRKSSHH

COME ON, LANTERN. *THE HOUSE OF MYSTERY* IS OUR *ONLY LEAD* ON FINDING OUT *WHERE* PHANTOM STRANGER TOOK BATMAN, KATANA AND DEADMAN.

THE STRANGER SAID THEY WERE GOING TO TALK TO *DOCTOR LIGHT* (WHO'S DEAD) AND HE DISAPPEARED WITH HALF OUR CREW.

SO KEEP TRYING TO GET US BACK IN.

IT'S *NOT* WORKING.

HAL COULD DO IT.

WHAT?

SORRY, IT JUST CAME OU

YES.

MORE THAN ANYTHING. I WAS HOPING--

I WAS HOPING YOU WOULD *TEACH* ME HOW.

I HAVE *ALREADY* BEEN TEACHING YOU. IF YOU WISH IT, I WILL TEACH YOU FOR MANY YEARS MORE. YOU *ARE* IMMORTAL.

WITH WHAT YOU ALREADY KNOW, AND WHAT YOU MAY YET LEARN, YOU WILL HAVE DIFFICULTY FINDING A FOE YOU COULD *NOT* KILL.

BUT A TIME WILL COME.

YOU WILL DRAW YOUR WEAPONS AT THE *FALL.* YOU WILL FACE THE *FLOOD...*

"...AND I PRAY
YOU WILL REMEMBER
MY WORDS."

THE HEROES OF THE
WORLD ARE AT WAR. THEY
BATTLE FOR THE PRIZE--
THE BOX THAT ONCE HELD
ALL THE SINS OF THE
WORLD, AND NOW HOLDS
THE KEY TO MY CURSE.

LOOK INTO THIS HERE.

THERE IS NO LIQUID IN THE BOWL. YOU ARE LOOKING AT A SLUMBERING *SPIRIT*.

VERY COMFORTABLE IN ITS LITTLE WOODEN BED! HAHA! I SANG IT A *LULLABY*.

YOU CANNOT *TOUCH* IT. YOU CANNOT *POUR* IT OR *CUT* IT OR *BURN* IT. BUT YOU CAN *SEE* YOURSELF IN IT, EH?

YOU CAN *SEE* YOURSELF IN IT.

WISDOM. ⊰HMPH⊱

SHALL WE BEGIN YOUR *LESSONS*?

I GOT NOTHING TO SAY.

NO? WE'RE NOT POLICE, MARCUS.

BUT WE *HAVE* HEARD OF YOU AND YOUR OPERATION-- YOUR CUSTOM GUNS AND WHATEVER.

SOME OF MY GOOD FRIENDS ARE *BUYERS* OF YOURS, ACTUALLY. I'M WITH S.H.A.D.E.

AW HELL. YOU KNOW I AIN'T *SUPERNATURAL.*

ROOM *FULL* OF ILLEGAL WEAPONS AND YOU DON'T EVEN KEEP YOUR DOOR LOCKED? YOU MUST HAVE A *HELL* OF A REPUTATION.

OR *POWERFUL* FRIENDS.

LIKE THIS WOMAN.

DO YOU RECOGNIZE HER?

I TOLD YOU, I GOT NOTHING TO SAY. YOU WANT INFO ON ME, WANT TO KNOW WHO MY FRIENDS ARE? S.H.A.D.E.'S GOT IT ALL.

AND I STILL HAVEN'T SEEN ANY I.D.

HOW'S THIS?

A.R.G.U.S... WHAT'S THAT?

RIGHT. I'M GOING TO GUESS YOU'VE BEEN HERE WORKING ALL DAY AND YOU HAVEN'T SEEN...

...THIS.

JESUS.

A.R.G.U.S. DEALS WITH *METAHUMANS*, MARCUS.

IT DIDN'T TAKE LONG FOR US TO FIGURE OUT THAT THE GUNS *PANDORA* CARRIES ARE YOUR CREATIONS.

THE GUNS AND ALL THE *OTHER* STUFF.

LOOKS LIKE WE'VE GOT A *PROBLEM*, HUH? I MEAN, POWERFUL FRIENDS ARE ONE THING--BUT THIS WOMAN'S A LISTED *SUPERVILLAIN.*

AND WE'RE GOING TO HAVE TO BRING YOU IN.

UNLESS YOU WANT TO TELL US RIGHT NOW...

OH. LEHRER, I UNDERSTAND NOW...

...WHAT YOU WERE TRYING TO *TELL* ME. I *SEE* MYSELF IN *THEM*.

DO YOU HEAR ME? MAYBE SOMETHING'S HAPPENED TO THE *BOX*. MAYBE SOMETHING'S HAPPENED TO *ME*.

I *SEE* MYSELF!

WHAT'S THIS? SOMETHING'S *CHANGED*...

ALL THESE MANY YEARS...ALL THE PEOPLE I GREW TO *KNOW*...

AND THEY WOULD *LIVE*, AND *LOVE*, AND GROW *OLD*. THEY, WHO COULD *LAUGH*, WHO COULD FIND *PEACE*...

WHO COULD BEAR *CHILDREN*... AND *DIE*...

SOMETHING'S *DIFFERENT* NOW... HOW *CURIOUS*...

"I AM XANADU AND I AM ALONE. I WAS TAKEN. HELD HERE IN THE DARK, BY EVIL MEN WITH EVIL PLANS.

AT FIRST I COULDN'T UNDERSTAND WHY THEY WANTED ME. OF ALL THE SUPER HUMANS CAUGHT UP IN THEIR MACHINATIONS, WHY DID I, SIMPLE CLAIRVOYANT, POSE SUCH A THREAT TO THESE MEN?

BUT NOW I KNOW. THEY DON'T WANT ME OUT OF THEIR GAME BECAUSE I CAN MOVE MOUNTAINS OR SHAKE THE EARTH...THEY NEED ME HERE BECAUSE I CAN SEE.

...I SEE EVERYTHING.

JEFF LEMIRE Writer
MIKEL JANIN Artist

I SEE THE MIGHTY FALL.

A.R.G.U.S., THE HUB OF THE JUSTICE LEAGUES, HAS BEEN DESTROYED... SUPERMAN AND HIS COMPANIONS CAUGHT IN THE CENTER OF THE APOCALYPTIC BLAST.

JEROMY COX Colorist • ROB LEIGH Letterer

I SEE THE GUILTY PUNISHED.

BATMAN AND HIS TEAM WENT ALL THE WAY TO HELL AND BACK TO LOOK FOR THE SECRETS THAT COME SO EASILY TO ME...AND INSTEAD FOUND THE PHANTOM STRANGER DESTROYED.

DOUG MAHNKE and ALEX SINCLAIR Cover

I SEE THE CON MAN, CAUGHT AT LAST.

JOHN CONSTANTINE, THE TRICKSTER, TRIED TO TAKE THE POWERFUL SHAZAM OUT OF THE GAME TO USE HIM FOR HIS OWN GAIN, AS CONSTANTINE IS ALWAYS WONT TO DO.

BUT IN THE YOUNG-HEARTED SHAZAM, CONSTANTINE MAY HAVE MET HIS MATCH AT LAST.

BUT ALL OF THIS IS JUST NOISE...

AND WHEN I LOOK PAST IT ALL, WHEN I BLOCK EVERYTHING ELSE OUT, I SEE THE REAL BATTLE AT THE HEART OF ALL THIS CHAOS...

DEADMAN, ARE YOU OKAY?!

I--I THINK SO, FLASH. FELT LIKE MY HEAD WAS GONNA EXPLODE THERE FOR A MINUTE... 'COURSE, I'M ALREADY DEAD, SO I GUESS TECHNICALLY THAT'S IMPOSSIBLE.

WHAT THE HELL WAS THAT, BRAND?

SOME KIND OF MAJOR DISTURBANCE IN THE MAGICAL PLAINS. AND I DO MEAN MAJOR.

RIPPED RIGHT THROUGH EVERYTHING. FOR A SECOND IT WAS LIKE EVERYTHING MAGICAL WAS INSIDE ME SCREAMING TO GET OUT...

I MEAN I COULD FEEL EVERYONE...ZATANNA, CONSTANTINE, EVEN SOME GUY WITH A GOLD HELMET I'D NEVER SEEN BEFORE.

...AND THAT NEW GUY, SHAZAM, HIM MOST OF ALL. I SENSED HIM AT THE HEART OF IT ALL.

SHAZAM?

WAIT A MINUTE, DEADMAN. YOU SAID YOU SENSED EVERYONE?

YES, I-- MADAME XANADU!

I THINK I CAN FIND HER!"

THOOM

WHAT THE HELL JUST HAPPENED?!

THE ENERGY READINGS FROM DR. LIGHT'S BODY WENT OFF THE CHARTS. I THINK--I THINK HE EXPLODED!

THEN WH AREN'T W TOAST?

WHAT IS IT, FIRESTORM?! IF YOU KNOW SOMETHING--

WALLER HAD ME LEARN HOW TO MAK KRYPTONITE. SHE TOLD ME IT WAS JUS A FAILSAFE, BUT--

ARE YOU KIDDING ME?! THESE WERE MY PEOPLE... MY FAMILY! YES, I HAD HIM MAKE KRYPTONITE, BECAUSE LIKE ALL OF YOU, I HAVE NO IDEA WHAT THE HELL HAPPENED TO SUPERMAN!

NOW, YOU CAN ALL STAND AROUND BLAMING ME LATER IF YOU WANT, BUT RIGHT NOW I'M GOING TO START LOOKING FOR SURVIVORS!

SHE'S RIGHT. THERE MAY STILL BE PEOPLE ALIVE HERE. WE NEED TO STOP FIGHTING AND HELP THEM!

YOU HEARD THE MAN...SEARCH AND RESCUE. MOVE!

MANHUNTER, STAY WITH SUPERMAN. ARROW, YOU KEEP THAT BOW ON WALLER.

I STILL DON'T BELIEVE A DAMNED WORD SHE'S SAYING.

HOLD IT RIGHT THERE!

I SEE IT!

EASY--

NO! TH--THEY TRIED TO KEEP ME BLIND...BUT I SAW IT! I SAW WHAT IT *REALLY* IS!

PANDORA WAS WRONG--YOU WERE ALL WRONG! IT'S NOT A PRISON...IT'S *A DOORWAY!*

SHE'S RIGHT. IT *IS* A DOORWAY...

ON THAT *SAME DAY*, WHILE THE BARRIERS BETWEEN UNIVERSES WERE WEAKENED, I FINALLY *ESCAPED* FROM WHAT WAS *LEFT* OF *MY* WORLD.

BUT MY MASTER DID NOT.

THEY DIDN'T MAKE IT.

THE JUSTICE LEAGUE CONTINUED TO BATTLE *OVERT THREATS* TO THE WORLD WHILE WE STAYED *HIDDEN*.

NO, MY DEAR, BUT WE DID.

HA.

AND SO MY MISSION TO SAVE HIM BEGAN.

WHEN I DISCOVERED THE *EXISTENCE* OF PANDORA'S BOX I FELT *HOPE*.

I *RECOGNIZED* IT.

I KNEW WHERE IT CAME FROM AND WHAT IT COULD DO.

I RECRUITED THE LEAGUE'S MANY ENEMIES, STARTING WITH *PROFESSOR IVO*.

FOR THE FIRST YEAR, I STRUGGLED TO COMPREHEND THE CULTURE AND RULES OF THIS BIZARRE PLACE.

EVEN THE VERY BASIC OF IDEAS APPEARED TWISTED AND TURNED INSIDE OUT.

EAST IS WEST AND WEST IS EAST.

WHILE THE LEAGUE CONTINUED ON, I SEARCHED FOR A WAY TO HELP THE MAN WHO RESCUED ME FROM MY DESTITUTE LIFE.

I HAD MANY MOMENTS OF DOUBT AND DESPERATION DURING THIS TIME.

I FELT ALONE.

BUT I REFUSED TO FAIL MY MASTER.

I BEGAN BUILDING THE *SECRET SOCIETY* TO BE AT THE READY FOR MY MASTER'S ARRIVAL.

THEN I PLANTED AN AGENT WITHIN THE JUSTICE LEAGUE'S RANKS.

AND WITH THE HIGH LEVEL OF *DISTRUST* BETWEEN THE LEAGUES, I KNEW IT WAS ONLY A MATTER OF TIME BEFORE OPPORTUNITY WOULD PRESENT ITSELF.

WHEN THE LEAGUES CAME INTO CONFLICT, I MADE THE WORLD BELIEVE SUPERMAN HAD KILLED ONE OF HIS WOULD-BE TEAMMATES. THEY THOUGHT IT TO BE BECAUSE OF HIS ENCOUNTER WITH *PANDORA'S BOX.*

SO THE LEAGUES SET OFF TO *FIND* IT. THEY'VE DONE MY JOB FOR ME.

HA.

I AM AN *OUTSIDER* TO THIS WORLD.

I AM *THE* OUTSIDER.

AND I SERVE MY MASTER WELL.

THIS ONE *WILL* BE OURS.

THEY BROUGHT THE BOX HERE, WONDER WOMAN. BACK TO WHERE I FIRST *FOUND* IT.

YOU NEED TO LET ME *HELP*--

YOU'VE HELPED *ENOUGH*, PANDORA.

WHAT'S WRONG, VIBE?

I'VE GOT ONE OF MY, *UH*, *"VIBE"* HEADACHES, FLASH...

...THERE'S SOMETHING THAT'S *NOT FROM OUR UNIVERSE* NEARBY. OR SOMEONE. MAYBE *BOTH*.

HE BLOODY THING *CORRUPTS* WHOEVER *TOUCHES* IT. 'CEPT FOR *ME*, RIGHT? I'M ALREADY *GOOD AN' GONE*.

ZEE?

IF MY FATHER WERE ALIVE, HE'D HAVE *KILLED* YOU FOR THE WAY YOU TREATED ME.

BUT *YOU* CAPES ON'T KNOW HOW TA EAL WITH THAT *DARK* CE CREEPING IN YOUR EADS. IT'S ALREADY GOT SHAZAM!

TELL 'EM, LUV. ZATANNA?

BLIMEY.

NOT YOU TOO.

EVIG EM EHT XOB!

GEOFF JOHNS WRITER

IVAN REIS PENCILLER

JOE PRADO, OCLAIR ALBERT & EBER FERREIRA INKERS

ROD REIS COLORS • **NICK J. NAPOLITANO** LETTERS

DOUG MAHNKE & ALEX SINCLAIR COVER

TRINITY **WAR** CONCLUSION

BATMAN'S GOT THE BOX! WE CAN HELP SUPERMAN--

YOU THINK I CARE ABOUT WHAT HAPPENS TO *SUPERMAN*, LANTERN?

HE *TOOK* DIANA FROM ME, SIMON. LET HIM *ROT*.

YOU'RE JUST A MAN.

I'M NOT *AFRAID* OF YOU, BATMAN. I'M THE *GREEN LANTERN*.

BUT YOU'RE *NO HAL* JORDAN.

HEY, *NEW GUY*.

THE BOX MIGHT BE MAKING ALL OF US A LITTLE *CRAZY* IN THE HEAD, BUT I DON'T THINK IT'S WHAT'S MAKING SUPERMAN *SICK.*

I DIDN'T SEE IT BEFORE BECAUSE IT'S SO *FAINT*, BUT...IT'S GETTING *STRONGER*.

I SEE IT TOO, RONNIE.

WHAT IS IT, FIRE-STORM?

SUPERMAN'S EMITTING SOME KIND OF *RADIOACTIVE AURA*... IT'S...

WE WOULDN'T HAVE RECOGNIZED IT WITHOUT WALLER'S HELP.

IT'S *KRYPTONITE.*

HE'S BEING *POISONED* BY *KRYPTONITE?* WHERE IS IT?

I THINK IT'S COMING FROM *INSIDE* SUPERMAN.

I CAN FIND IT.

I CAN TURN INTO *OXYGEN* AND ENTER HIS *BLOOD-STREAM.* THEN TRACE THE *DYING CELLS* BACK TO THE SOURCE.

IT... IT'S IN HIS *BRAIN.*

HIS *BRAIN?*

THERE'S A *MICROSCOPIC SLIVER* OF *KRYPTONITE* IN THERE.

HOW'D A MICROSCOPIC SLIVER OF KRYPTONITE GET *IN HIS BRAIN?*

OH, THAT'S AN *EASY QUESTION* TO ANSWER, CYBORG.

I PUT IT
IN THERE.

YOU?

"WHEN WE WERE GOING
UP AGAINST THE JLA--"

"--I WENT INTO SUPERMAN'S BRAIN
WITH THE SLIVER OF KRYPTONITE I
TOOK FROM BATMAN'S RING.

"I HIT A
NERVE...

"...AND
TRIGGERED
HIS HEAT
VISION."

I KNOW YOU
THOUGHT I WAS PART
OF THE JUSTICE
LEAGUE--AND THE JLA
THINKS I WORK FOR
THEM, BUT THE TRUTH
IS I DON'T WORK FOR
ANY OF YOU.

IT'S OURS.

KKRRAKKKZZTTTT

WHOEVER YOU ARE, YOU CAN'T YAAHH!

IT'S TOO LATE, FLASH.

I DON'T UNDERSTAND.

YOU NEVER DID, PANDORA. SINCE THE GODS WHO DAMNED YOU FIRST FOUND THIS BOX, THEY BELIEVED IT TO BE MAGIC. BUT THEY WERE WRONG.

IT'S SCIENCE.

VARIANT COVER GALLERY

TRINITY OF SIN: PANDORA 1
Variant cover by Pasqual Ferry & Brad Anderson

JUSTICE LEAGUE 22
Variant cover by Brett Booth, Norm Rapmund & Andrew Dalhouse

JUSTICE LEAGUE DARK 22
Variant cover by Brett Booth, Norm Rapmund & Andrew Dalhouse

JUSTICE LEAGUE OF AMERICA 6
Variant cover by Brett Booth, Norm Rapmund & Andrew Dalhouse

JUSTICE LEAGUE OF AMERICA 7
Variant cover by Mikel Janin, Vicente Cifuentes & Tomeu Morey

JUSTICE LEAGUE DARK 23
Variant cover by Mikel Janin, Vicente Cifuentes & Tomeu Morey

JUSTICE LEAGUE 23
Variant cover by Mikel Janin, Vicente Cifuentes & Tomeu Morey

"Welcoming to new fans looking to get into superhero comics for the first time and old fans who gave up on the funny-books long ago."
—SCRIPPS HOWARD NEWS SERVICE

START AT THE BEGINNING!

JUSTICE LEAGUE VOLUME 1: ORIGIN

AQUAMAN
VOLUME 1:
THE TRENCH

THE SAVAGE
HAWKMAN VOLUME 1:
DARKNESS RISING

GREEN ARROW
VOLUME 1:
THE MIDAS TOUCH

GEOFF **JOHNS** JIM **LEE** SCOTT **WILLIAMS**

© 2012 DC Comics. All Rights Reserved.

DC COMICS™

"If you don't love it from the very first page
you're not human.*
—MTV GEEK

"ANIMAL MAN has the sensationa.
Jeff Lemire at the helm.*
—ENTERTAINMENT WEEKLY

START AT THE BEGINNING!

ANIMAL MAN
VOLUME 1: THE HUNT

JUSTICE LEAGUE DARK
VOLUME 1:
IN THE DARK

RESURRECTION MAN
VOLUME 1:
DEAD AGAIN

FRANKENSTEIN
AGENT OF S.H.A.D.E.
VOLUME 1: WAR OF
THE MONSTERS

VOLUME 1
THE HUNT

"TRAVEL FOREMAN'S ART
IS INNOVATIVE AND
EXCELLENTLY CREEPY...
AS LEMIRE'S EVERYMAN
HERO MAKES HIS MARK IN
THE NEW DC UNIVERSE."

— USA TODAY

JEFF LEMIRE TRAVEL FOREMAN

Cuyahoga Falls
Library
Cuyahoga Falls, Ohio

JUSTICE LEAGUE
TRINITY WAR

GEOFF **JOHNS** RAY **FAWKES**
JEFF **LEMIRE** J.M. **DEMATTEIS** writers

IVAN **REIS** MIKEL **JANIN**
DOUG **MAHNKE** DANIEL **SAMPERE**
RENATO **GUEDES** FERNANDO **BLANCO**
CHRISTIAN **ALAMY** OCLAIR **ALBERT** ZANDER **CANNON**
KEITH **CHAMPAGNE** VICENTE **CIFUENTES** MARC **DEERING**
EBER **FERREIRA** GENE **HA** JIM **LEE** TOM **NGUYEN**
JOE **PRADO** KENNETH **ROCAFORT** WALDEN **WONG**
SCOTT **WILLIAMS** PATRICK **ZIRCHER** artists

BRAD **ANDERSON** BLOND JEROMY **COX** GABE **ELTAEB**
NATHAN **EYRING** HI-FI ART **LYON** MARCELO **MAIOLO**
PETE **PANTAZIS** ROD **REIS** ALEX **SINCLAIR** colorists

SAL **CIPRIANO** TAYLOR **ESPOSITO** TRAVIS **LANHAM** ROB **LEIGH**
CARLOS M. **MANGUAL** NICK J. **NAPOLITANO** DEZI **SIENTY** letterers

JIM **LEE**, SCOTT **WILLIAMS** AND ALEX **SINCLAIR** collection cover artists

SUPERMAN created by JERRY **SIEGEL** & JOE **SHUSTER**
by special arrangement with the Jerry Siegel family

EDDIE BERGANZA DAN DIDIO WIL MOSS BRIAN CUNNINGHAM Editors – Original Series
HARVEY RICHARDS Associate Editor – Original Series KATE STEWART Assistant Editor – Original Series
PETER HAMBOUSSI Editor ROBBIN BROSTERMAN Design Director – Books ROBBIE BIEDERMAN Publication Design

BOB HARRAS Senior VP – Editor-in-Chief, DC Comics

DIANE NELSON President DAN DIDIO and JIM LEE Co-Publishers
GEOFF JOHNS Chief Creative Officer
JOHN ROOD Executive VP – Sales, Marketing and Business Development
AMY GENKINS Senior VP – Business and Legal Affairs NAIRI GARDINER Senior VP – Finance
JEFF BOISON VP – Publishing Planning MARK CHIARELLO VP – Art Direction and Design
JOHN CUNNINGHAM VP – Marketing TERRI CUNNINGHAM VP – Editorial Administration
ALISON GILL Senior VP – Manufacturing and Operations HANK KANALZ Senior VP – Vertigo and Integrated Publishing
JAY KOGAN VP – Business and Legal Affairs, Publishing JACK MAHAN VP – Business Affairs, Talent
NICK NAPOLITANO VP – Manufacturing Administration SUE POHJA VP – Book Sales
COURTNEY SIMMONS Senior VP – Publicity BOB WAYNE Senior VP – Sales

JUSTICE LEAGUE: TRINITY WAR

Published by DC Comics. Copyright © 2014 DC Comics. All Rights Reserved.

Originally published in single magazine form as JUSTICE LEAGUE 22-23, JUSTICE LEAGUE OF AMERICA 6-7,
JUSTICE LEAGUE DARK 22-23, TRINITY OF SIN: PANDORA 1-3, TRINITY OF SIN: PHANTOM STRANGER 11,
CONSTANTINE 5, NEW 52 FREE COMIC BOOK DAY SPECIAL 2012 © 2012, 2013 DC Comics. All Rights Reserved.
All characters, their distinctive likenesses and related elements featured in this publication are trademarks of DC Comics.
The stories, characters and incidents featured in this publication are entirely fictional.
DC Comics does not read or accept unsolicited ideas, stories or artwork.

DC Comics, 1700 Broadway, New York, NY 10019
A Warner Bros. Entertainment Company.
Printed by RR Donnelley, Salem, VA, USA. 2/7/14. First Printing.

HC ISBN: 978-1-4012-4519-1
SC ISBN: 978-1-4012-4944-1

Library of Congress Cataloging-in-Publication Data

Johns, Geoff, 1973-
Justice League : Trinity War / Geoff Johns, Jeff Lemire.
pages cm.— (The New 52!)
Summary: "The event that the New 52 has been building towards since the beginning! #1 New York Times best-selling writer Geoff Johns (Green
Lantern, Batman: Earth One) brings together almost two years of plot threads here in Justice League: Trinity War. When the three Justice Leagues
go to war with one another, who's side will everyone be on? Allies will be born, friends will become enemies, and the DC Universe will never be the
same! This hardcover graphic novel collects Free Comic Book Day 2012, Trinity of Sin: Pandora #1-3, Trinity of Sin: Phantom Stranger #11, Justice
League #22-23, Justice League Dark #22-23, Justice League of America #6-7, and Constantine #5"— Provided by publisher.
ISBN 978-1-4012-4519-1 (hardback)
1. Graphic novels. I. Lemire, Jeff. II. Title. III. Title: Trinity War.
PN6728.J87J6558 2014
741.5'973—dc23
2013045590

 SUSTAINABLE
FORESTRY
INITIATIVE

Certified Chain of Custody
At Least 20% Certified Forest Content
www.sfiprogram.org
SFI-01042
APPLIES TO TEXT STOCK ONLY